WIWAK
When I Was A Kid

M. E. Tasker

Mystical Rose Press

"WIWAK - When I Was A Kid"

By M.E. Tasker

Published in the United States of America
First Published 2012
ISBN 978-0-615-434971-1

Editors	Jeannette Williams
	Christine Koziol
Cover Art	Alex Miklowski
Layout	Miko Gandhi Paulin

This book is dedicated to Saint Katharine Drexel for her intervention in my life, and the many blessings she continues to bestow on me.

Acknowledgments

I want to thank my son, John, and my wife, Maureen, for their encouragement during the creation of this book. My harshest critics, both frankly informed me what ideas were gold, and those that were clunkers. I don't want to thank everyone I ever met in my life, but I do want to acknowledge my mother, Anna, who is a lifelong inspiration to me on many fronts.

Next, I would like to acknowledge all the guidance, assistance and understanding afforded to me by Publisher Cathy Walsh. She is a genuine individual and a personal inspiration to me.

Kudos also go out to Editors Christine Koziol and Jeanette Williams. Both women helped me organize my script and made suggestions that enhanced the book itself.

Special thanks to my nephew, Matthew Tasker, for showing me the real meaning of perseverance on a daily basis.

Thanks to Artist Alex Miklowski for her creative work on the cover.

Also to Miko Gandhi Paulin for his work on the layout and his other technical expertise that he used to make this book "sing."

Table of Contents

Introduction

"When I was a kid, the Dead Sea was just
sick, and water was free!"

Back in those days old geezers would begin everything
they said with five words, "When I Was A Kid..."
I'm positive geezers have been using the same line
since time immemorial. Things have changed at such a
phenomenal rate in America the past fifty years that I
now find myself echoing the chorus of geezers I ridiculed.
It's safe to say it's a common malady with adults that, when
gazing back over the long distance of time, the old days always
seem better. Many books have been written about the age of
the Baby Boomers (born 1946 through
1964), but few have actually examined
the real life of the "average Joe"
and his family. Stereotypes abound
in books, television, and movies,
but none are completely accurate.

Mike Tasker-Age 4

After World War II concluded,
millions of military servicemen
returned from the world conflict and
the inevitable happened: after long, lonely years spent with
millions of men, they eagerly found pretty wives and began
making babies – millions and millions of babies! The Baby

1

Boom Generation was born literally, and I was one of them! I lived among the natives and would like to now reveal the good, the bad, and the weird things these kids did.

When Johnny came marching home, my father, Thomas Charles Tasker, came home in one piece to West Philadelphia, Pennsylvania. Awaiting him at his row home on 44th and Market Street were his wife, Anna, and two sons, Thomas and Robert.

In the ensuing seven years this Navy veteran, who had witnessed the carnage of the

Thomas and Anna Tasker

Pacific Theater for three years aboard two destroyers (U.S.S. Sauflee and the U.S.S. Hudson), was anxious to resume his normal life. He picked up where he left off and sired three more children: Anna Regina, Charles, and me – the last in this litter of five. My dad worked for Railroad Express Company. Our neighborhood fame came when Dad bought one of the first televisions made available in the late 1940s. My brothers suddenly had a lot of new pals. Each weekday my father would go off to work and mother would manage the roost. Neither parent knew how to drive a car and depended on public transportation, or their God-given legs. The houses in the neighborhood were in decent shape, but were plagued by roaches. Every so often Dad would have to "bomb" (insecticide) the house, while my mom took us to the Philadelphia Zoo, the oldest zoo in America, on a day when they offered free admission.

Each weekday my brothers and sister would walk four times to St. James Catholic School, which was ten blocks away on 38th and Chestnut Street. Children were allowed to come home for an hour lunch. When not in school, both boys played on Ludlow Street, and it wasn't long before both were hit by cars, once each, and hospitalized. Even though the open grounds of Drexel University were across Market Street from our house, my mother wanted more open space and areas for her kids to play safely. She longed for a house like the one her father, John Lynch, had built in Horsham, Pa., on Avenue A in Montgomery County. Her father, a policeman, raised his family at 20th & Lombard in Philadelphia, but built the country house back in the 1920's mainly as a place for his 10 children to escape the summer heat of the city.

One August day in 1953, my father hopped a train to Bristol, Pa., and arrived back home at 10 p.m. to inform my mother to pack her bags. He had bought a new home for $8,900 on a $100 deposit in a new place called Levittown. Levittown, located thirty miles north of Philadelphia and bordering the same Delaware River George Washington crossed on that cold Christmas day in 1776, was the second mass suburban housing development built by the "Father of Suburbia," William Jaird Levitt. From 1952 to 1957, Levitt, his father, Abraham, and brother, Alfred built the development from the ground up in an area that encompassed twenty-two square miles. My father purchased a rancher, one of six housing models found within the 5,500 acres of land. Our house was one of 17,311 units that held slightly over 70,000 residents in 41 sections.

Prospective buyers waiting to view new Levittown model homes -1951*

We moved into the family home on my mother's birthday, and she truly believed it was a miracle. The name of our street in the North Park section was aptly named Nature Lane. My father carried his wife over the threshold, and my brothers and sister quickly flooded in from behind into our American dream.

Levitt's vision of the perfect planned American community was a dream-come-true for both him and the Tasker clan. The house, which featured water faucets that mixed hot and cold water, was like some science fiction house of the future

*Photo courtesy of Urban Archives, Temple University

for my brothers and sister. The second floor of the house was not completely finished, but the new arrivals said they didn't mind. The stove was electric and there was oil heat that permeated through the concrete floors. In the back yards each house had a couple fruit trees from the 48,000 trees Levitt's men planted. We had nectarine, apple, and pear trees that produced fruit for decades. The apple tree still survives and gives luscious fruit for pies and cakes each fall. And no one could believe that they could swim in an Olympic-sized pool all summer long for a family membership fee of $6. Not a shabby deal for a family of seven. We really believed we had landed somewhere over the rainbow, as Judy Garland had in Oz only fourteen years earlier in 1939.

Even though my older brothers missed some of their friends from the city, they quickly adapted and made new friends with the other transplanted kids hailing primarily from New Jersey, New York, and Delaware. No matter where you went, the place was crawling with kids, overflowing out the doors and into the streets. There were 171 miles of new road to play on, and huge fields for baseball and other games. Trips back to the old neighborhood got fewer and fewer as time went by.

Everything just kept getting better, until my father was diagnosed with cancer in 1955. In the blink of an eye the Lord took him from us and we buried him at Holy Cross Cemetery in Yeadon, Pa., which is also known as the "Irish Racetrack." My courageous mother never missed a beat in raising us and paying off a 30-year mortgage. She never remarried, and would answer all queries on her marital status by simply saying, "Why marry again, when I've had the best?" Through prayer, family, and friends we met in Levittown, we prospered and made a good life for ourselves.

My father died when I was three-and-a-half years old. I am the only child in my family who has no recollection of my father. I never had the chance to toss a ball, share a laugh, or take a swim with him. Many men I met over the years through sports and friends were wonderful to me, and I thank God for sending them my way. When these men passed away, I cried as if I lost a family member. But it wasn't quite the same. My mother would often tell us, "You don't miss what you don't have," but my mother always knew it didn't apply to my father.

Yet, my loss left me with a certain maturity other kids lacked. From an early age I would admonish friends who didn't appreciate their fathers. I told them they should be thankful for what they had. I'm certain my dad will have two baseball mitts ready, and be standing first in line to greet me when I cross over to the other side. Despite Eric Clapton's poignant song "Tears In Heaven," I'm betting my father will know my name, and we'll catch up on a lot of lost time – fifty-seven years and counting.

My mother lied to us and told us she had finished high school. She assured us we would all graduate, even if it killed her. All of us graduated, and my brother, Robert, and I earned extra college degrees, or as "me Irish mother" liked to call it, "icing on the cake". We excelled in all facets of private and public schools, and Robert and Charles won state championships in diving and track respectively, while

Tom captured a Duncan Yo-Yo championship. My sister, Jean, was an excellent student and a great help to me with my homework.

After graduating from Pennsbury High School in Fairless Hills, Pa., I landed a sports writing job for the Bucks County Courier Times in Levittown. Next, I attended college full time at Trenton State College in New Jersey. Later, I attended graduate school, taught English at my old high school (Pennsbury), and married my wife, Maureen, who gave me a son, John. We

The Clan-(bottom row, from left) Author Mike Tasker and Jean; (second row, from left) Charles, Tom and Bob.

named him after my wife's father, who passed away five months after he was born. We happily live in the same section of Levittown (North Park) that was my boyhood home.

They (nobody knows who 'they' really are) say it's not the destination, but the journey that truly counts in life. This book addresses what it was like to grow up among the first wave of Baby Boomers in the nation's largest suburban development at that time. Books have been penned about the period, but most, if not all, fail to get down to the nitty-gritty of the everyday kid on the streets. These Levittown kids represent a microcosm of what Baby Boomers were doing all across America.

7

To My Audience:

To Baby Boomers, I hope this book allows you to sit back and laugh, yes laugh, about a place in time that now seems like it is somewhere over that rainbow. A place you wouldn't believe existed had you not been part of it. A land of Easy Bake Ovens and chemical sets that marked their users with permanent reminders of their inquisitive youth.

To their children, I hope this book fills an important niche that has been up to now forgotten. It gives answers to kids from Generation X who wonder exactly what did children do without all the electronic wizardry that exists today. It shows kids their parents and grandparents possessed imaginations which allowed them to fill each and every new day with games and experiences that border on genius – even though most geniuses are a tad kooky. It lets kids know there's a lot of fun to be had outside of the house after school with other kids, not holed up in a room with their computers. It finally explains why Uncle Billy has only three fingers on his left hand, sports a glass eyeball, has more scars than Frankenstein, walks with the assistance of a cane, can't hear, and keeps repeating to anyone who will listen to him – "Watch out! It's gonna blow!"

To social historians, this is a narrative of kids who will never get their 15 minutes of fame. It allows a new look at what Boomers created for themselves in their youth, and provides possible clues to what they intend

8

to do as they redefine growing old. Boomers officially began retiring in 2011 and represent over 11.6 trillion dollars in inheritances. This fact alone means a lot of people will continue to cater to their wants and needs before they walk off the American stage. I suggest the Boomers still remain a work in progress; a generation that still doesn't follow conventional wisdom. Some things the Boomers did in their youth are familiar to kids today, while a large majority of things they pulled off border on sheer lunacy – they would label it genius.

Yes, ladies and gentlemen, boys and girls, "Mr. & Mrs. America," and all the ships at sea – this book recalls a time when pretentious windbags in the media didn't have all the answers to every possible subject in America. It's a time when not one rat study had been completed by scientists for anything that proved to be cancerous if consumed on a daily basis; a time when four-out-of-five dentists hadn't been asked about which leading brand of toothpaste, cigarettes, or coffee they preferred; a time when inexpensive box cameras recorded the daily goings-on of this unique generation in grainy black and white images; a time that beckons us to really look at how 70-plus million boys and girls came of age in a unique time in world history – a time When I Was A Kid!

Chapter 1

You Did What!!!

"Either write something worth reading or do something worth writing."

Benjamin Franklin

WIWAK games we played were at times very dangerous. We would have told stuntmen, if we would have known any, not to try the games at home. One game that would get us arrested today was a game entitled, "Dodge the Arrow!" The goal was quite simple: dodge an arrow! The rules: shoot an arrow up into the air, dodge it on its return to earth, or seek safe haven under a carport. Last one to run under the carport got one point. Those who stood out in harm's way could pick up valuable additional points. First person who stayed alive and compiled 10 points was declared the winner. Once a contestant misjudged a speedy arrow returning to earth, and sustained an arrow through his Chuck Taylors and a trip to the hospital. Local legend, Crazy Charlie (name changed to protect the insane), always won because he never moved once the game started. He always pushed the limits on any dare. His only loss ever came on a drug binge in the late 60's. Someone slipped a golden arrow next to his Nehru jacket at his funeral.

WIWAK removing expended flash bulbs from cameras required quick hands. Quite a few kids got burnt handling them, and a lot of furniture got singed from those movie camera aficionados using "sun guns." As kids we swore the sun gun was actually brighter than the sun itself. It's always a blast to look back at films from the 50's and 60's with subjects shielding their eyes like some giant star in a galaxy was blowing up five feet away from them. It's not stretching the truth to say the wires guarding the sun gun nova actually glowed red after prolonged use. Besides almost burning down the house, disfiguring junior's hands for life, giving sis a permanent sun burn, and melting PopPop's eyes, the stun gun's passage into history came quickly to avert possible lawsuits.

WIWAK we weren't happy just to ride down the street on our bikes doing about 50 mph and hitting the brakes on the cycles as hard as we could. The object to this scary trick was to see which kid could create the longest rubber skid on the road. We weren't just happy looking at the skids; sometimes we'd get out a yardstick and make a game of it by measuring who was the king of the skids. Many a Evel Knievel suffered scrapes and bruises when the bike went out of control and the unfortunate driver flew head first over the handlebars. Dentists in our neighborhood especially liked this game for their practice.

WIWAK and began smoking like my Uncle Jim, we played a game called "Smoke Out!" Contestants sat in a car with the windows up smoking their brains out. No air conditioning was allowed in summer; no heat in winter. The winner was the nitwit who could remain in the car the longest. In the summer, the eventual winner emerged from a cloud of smoke soaked in sweat, to the applause of those who bailed out during the heat of battle. A deviation of this game involved turning the car heater on in the middle of August to see who could withstand torrid heat the longest. And in winter, opening the car windows in January helped determine who "Chilly King" was. Nobody ever accused us of having above average intelligence, or common sense!

WIWAK some of the older boys in the neighborhood showed us youngsters that getting older didn't necessarily require huge amounts of brain tissue in their craniums. One game that mesmerized us was a little number they called "Hot Butts." The game was simple —two competitors would place a lit cigarette between their joined arms, and the winner would be determined by the person who did not pull away.

Guys who regularly played this game later were the first to get arms tattooed at a local carnival. Only sailors, truckers, and bikers got tattoos back then.

WIWAK snow during the winter did not stop the wheels turning in kids' minds. One popular game in Levittown, Pa., was jumping out the second story window of our houses. A crazy stunt? Yes indeed. However, a close second look revealed our stunt was not as dangerous as it first appears. Most of the $8,900 ranchers built by William Levitt in the early 1950s sat in sections without any trees or brush to stop drifting winter snows. It was not unusual for drifts to reach to the second floors among the 17,500 original homes that were built. Neighborhood snowball warlords could only build so many igloos and snow trails. Many realistic gunfights and death scenes took place in and out of second story windows while the kids were dressed up as cowboys (Wyatt Earp, Lucas McCoy, and Matt Dillon, etc.) Good guys and bad guys would actually stop shooting each other to watch any participant take a fall from above. It's a crying shame we didn't have the technology to film these stunts back then. Maybe more people would believe that this actually happened.

WIWAK one strange game played on a regular basis was "Hot Peas and Butter." It had absolutely nothing to do with food. The rules had one kid hiding a belt from a group of several boys in set boundaries. Next, the boy who found the belt was now allowed to chase and whip the other boys' backsides, but only when they left a set base. Sadistic yes, but for some unknown reason we couldn't get enough of the game and laughed our heads off each time we played it.

13

Some parents actually watched and laughed too when their offspring got the strap. My brother tried to lessen the sting of the beating by putting Marvel comic books in his pants. They found out his trick and beat him even more. Why we got a kick out of seeing other kids scream in pain is still a mystery to me.

WIWAK tough boys played a little game entitled "Knuckles". This game required two decks of playing cards, a sadistic sense of humor, and a strong desire to see blood. One player extended a hand holding tightly onto a deck of cards with three fingers. The opponent would then swing his deck of cards at the hand and try to dislodge the cards. The number of cards that dropped determined how many times your hands would be smacked again. Drop 10 cards and the back of your hand would be in for 10 smacks. At this point the game got interesting. The person doing the smacking would then select his method of hits with the deck. Chops, fashioning the deck like an ax blade, were worth 10 smacks of the hand; slams, smashing hand lying flat on table, garnered 5 points; and slices, fan cards to scrape knuckles, were worth two points. It didn't take long for the contest to draw blood from both combatants. The winner was determined by who could withstand the pain the longest. Needless to say, Band-Aids went quickly at home.

WIWAK a water hose turned on outside of the house meant someone was getting soaked, no matter what the season. Some would try to get away from the hose and climb on the roof of the house. My brother would turn off the nozzle, enter the house with the hose, and come out a window, soaking the cowards. We all looked up to my older brother. As the youngest in my family I thought of Tom as some kind of genius. I believed he caught some of Einstein's molecules from the water he drank. Although Einstein's ashes were spread at an undisclosed location, we all believed they were sprinkled into the Delaware, and that my brother had consumed them.

WIWAK part of growing up was getting the following tortures freely given to you by siblings, friends or drunken uncles: eye gouges, ear rubs, wet willies, knuckle rubs, wrist ringers and beard rubs. The effects of these tricks showed up later in life. Maladies from these have appeared in Boomers with cornea displacement, hearing aids, facial surgery lifts, carpal tunnel syndrome, male pattern baldness, and a knot on the head that never really went away. When I got older, I practiced this fine art on helpless kids, especially my nephews. It took decades to get even with my brothers through their kids. Oh sweet revenge.

WIWAK my best friend's father had guns and rifles of all kinds. Coming from a house whose only assault weapon was a fly swatter, I never tired of him showing me the extensive collection. His dad didn't believe in hiding the guns, and his son would have never bothered to take out the arms if I hadn't bugged him to. One day my buddy decided to try on his father's six guns and cowboy hat. He looked really sharp until his dad came in unexpectedly from work that same summer afternoon. My friend's face went white, and his dad looked at me and pointed to the door. His father never said anything about the incident to either of us for the rest of his life. Upon his passing, my friend inherited all his firearms. Later, I asked him whatever happened to those six-shooters his dad owned. He told me his father sold them the day after he was caught showing them off to me.

WIWAK my three older brothers always let me know they were the bosses. I still have the "accidental" scars on my body to this day. My brothers and I actually held "Friday Night Fights," when my mom stepped out to go to church sodality. We used towels around our fists for gloves, but all of my fights were chalked up for the loss column. Ninety-nine percent of them were called on account of "tears." My brother would make me madder by laughing when I swung at him for beating me up. Being the baby of the family was tough when mom wasn't around.

WIWAK we would actually scream at people for driving their automobiles down our street and interrupting our games being held throughout the year. We would usually scream, "What do you think this is, a road?" Some brazen kids would bump the car and act like they had been injured. Some were good actors and writhed in agony on the asphalt.

WIWAK delinquents I knew had knives of all shapes and sizes. The neatest one, that bestowed on the holder instant teen stature, was the switchblade. Some of these shanks would have made movie star Sal Mineo proud. When we weren't practicing throwing them into doors or sheds, the most popular game we played was "Chew the Peg," or "Mumbly Peg." The game involved flipping a pocket knife off each finger of the hand, arm, elbow and chin. Each time the knife had to land upright in the ground to proceed. Last one to finish the sequence had to chew a small peg of wood stuck in the dirt. The winners would make the task as difficult as possible by leaving just a small bit of wood exposed above ground. Nobody wanted to lose and wind up with brown and green teeth.

WIWAK an intriguing habit surfaced among some of the children on the streets of Levittown in the good ol' summertime. There were a few of us that favored chewing the tar that bubbled up on the streets in hot weather. Kids would actually search them out, pick them off the street and chew on them like Double Bubble gum. These were normal kids that weren't being denied food by their parents, and are still alive and pillars of society today. Other treats they loved to gnaw on also included Ju Ju Beads, Juicy Fruits, and rock candy. You might not be able to be understood by your friends, or you might lose a tooth, but this candy didn't leave your teeth with a noticeable black tint.

WIWAK I loved to stick my head into a grocery store freezer, especially during the hot summer days. I guess I loved the smell of the coolant chemicals (Freon) circulating around the frozen peas and corn. While I never turned into a huffing coke-addict, I still sneak a whiff now and then. I also liked the smells of diesel fuel from busses and boats, fresh cut grass in the summer time, leaves rotting and burning in the fall, old country stores, grandma's house, Christmas trees in the living room, and Vicks Vapor Rub on my chest when I was sick with a bad chest cold. It's really amazing how certain smells can take Boomers back in time.

WIWAK blowing objects through plastic straws was a

favorite pastime. A plastic straw and inexpensive navy beans or corn kernels were all that you needed to get started for days of fun. The games we played back then were similar to paintball games today – only $450 cheaper. However, the object of the game was the same – injure and create huge welts on your opponents' bodies. Shooting one pea, or letting go with a machine gun burst, required skills that took time to perfect. The most common problem in pea shooters occurred when your choice of ammo jammed in the tube. Such problems in the heat of battle could invite a full frontal attack from the enemy. One thing about our games is that we never really knew who won, since the games occurred over weeks. After we tired of the games and put our pea shooters on the shelf, we never gave a second thought to our expended ammo; that is until corn and pea plants began sprouting in the most unusual places the following spring.

WIWAK a whole lot of kids were firebugs. Older kids were constantly shooting matches at one another for fun. Kids who could light wooden matches off their jacket zipper or teeth were looked up to. Some kids became very creative with their pyrotechnic skills and utilized charcoal lighter fluid to write their names in fire on lawns. The truly crazy among us, Chucky, would take a can of hair spray, push the nozzle, and light the spray with a match creating a mini flame-thrower. Chucky also told us what hairspray can was the best to use doing this stunt. Where Chucky found the time to learn all these illuminating tricks amazed us to no end.

WIWAK plopping down 10 cents for a balsa wood

airplane would accord us countless hours of pleasure. These planes could do all kinds of stunts just by positioning the wings in different ways and throwing them into the air. Of course, some kids were better at it than others, and they let us know it. When the planes finally lost their appeal, a Black Cat firecracker attached to the body of the plane would supply an exciting ending in a flash of exploding balsa wood. Some older kids, however, weren't satisfied with blowing up their planes with firecrackers. They wanted the plane to blow up into dust, so they attached cherry bombs for a particularly loud finale.

WIWAK "Buck-Buck" was a game that required no assembly; only a few boys wishing to inflict pain on friends. The one item necessary to help begin the fun was a light pole. After dividing up sides between a dozen boys, one group would line up and hug onto a pole and each other. The opposing nitwits would then try to break up the pole group by running and jumping on their backs. During the jumps the pole huggers could try and buck off the other players. Points were tallied each way. This game was one of the few times it paid to have the fattest kid on the block. Also, care had to be taken when gauging jumps. Some players got too eager in their desire to inflict pain and wound up jumping too far and hitting their heads on the pole in the process. Chiropractors today should have a block for "Buck-Buck" on their pre-admission forms for patients who believe their back injuries stem back to this friendly childhood game.

WIWAK playing a pickup game of baseball was a daily ritual in my neighborhood. Boys of all ages were on both teams, yet deciding who got first bat was usually a bone of contention. The issue was finally settled with two of the older boys taking turns holding a baseball bat with two fingers, while the other kid tried to kick it out of his hand. It was a best of three for both sides. Whoever held onto the bat the most times after the kicks got to bat first. It's amazing the way we decided things without any intrusions from adults.

WIWAK we played football during the fall without pads and helmets. Quite a few games ended with kids in the hospital with fractured bones, but that didn't stop us from our play on the gridiron.

WIWAK we'd often clear off a basketball court after a snowstorm to play. Fingers might get cold if we stopped running for a long period, but we didn't care. Playing football in the snow was another favorite. Snowball fights would last for days and some sick kids would put stones and dirt in snowballs to hurt other combatants.

WIWAK a game that everyone played before it was time to go home each night was Hide & Seek. It made no difference how old one was, everyone was asked to play the game. It was neat being in a game with older kids. Any other time they would prohibit us from playing with them. Boundaries were set before each game, and my brother Charles was especially good at hiding. However, we later found out that he would sneak into the house and go to the bathroom when the game commenced.

WIWAK thumb wrestling was a very competitive sport. It ranked right up there with arm wrestling. Guys and gals were always testing each other to see who was the strongest.

WIWAK - When I Was A Kid

The toughest arm wrestler in our group was a girl. Not one guy could pin her.

Chapter 2

Memorable Lists

*"For the first time ever I was taking my
family on the road. We stayed with my in-
laws, which on life's list of experiences ranks
right below sitting in a tub full of scissors."*
Jeff Foxworthy

G rowing up in a town literally crawling with hordes of
unsupervised kids is something experts today would
deem wholly unacceptable. Yet, with all the children that
each family had, the poor Moms were glad to kick a few of

the older ones outdoors, since the fathers were not expected back home until after five o'clock. But whenever I wanted to join my older brother, he had to assure my mother that he would watch me closely. Once, though, he lost me at a crowded Saturday matinee featuring "Atlantis: The Lost Continent." I was catapulted through the movie theater door as kids pushed and shoved to get in. My brother, who never got to see the movie, walked home and cried to my mother that he "lost" me. Meanwhile, I sat in the theater watching the flick.

Summertime was the period of the year when we all explored what was beyond our section. Most of us traveled in groups. Taking Mom's advice, some kids didn't go back home until supper time, while others gladly ate over at a friend's house. While there was the occasional fight among boys, they were infrequent. Fighting was watched by those on hand, but combatants usually utilized fists and the fights were over when the other boy gave in. Good friends usually wrestled each other. Their fights came to a conclusion when the winner asked the loser to say, "Uncle." Surprisingly, the fighters usually knew each other, and made up soon afterwards. In most areas kids visited they were over-crowded with others playing various sports on a limited amount of playing space. Challenges by one group of kids against others always played out on the athletic fields. Most kids didn't know it at the time, but playing others who were much older made them all better athletes. The games and social interaction didn't end on the fields of play. Most times in the evenings, talk would turn to things that were on some of the kids' minds. Subjects included things that young boys and girls in this human incubator called Levittown deemed important. Coming up with lists of one kind or another was a daily occurrence. Lists could be both funny and alarming when compared with today's way of doing things in a politically correct society. No matter what, time flew by as we compiled the lists. Some included the following:

WIWAK movies, like baseball and boxing, were something boys always talked and argued about. We weren't just happy to see a movie. No, we had to debate its merits and what we would have done differently. One movie I'll never forget arguing about was the 1939 film classic, "Wizard of Oz." We all agreed we liked it, but thought that some of Dorothy's behavior should have been dealt with by Kansas police upon her return. This, we believed, would have made a better ending. Several of us actually wrote down in a copybook the charges that should have been lodged against her upon her return flight from the Land of Oz. Some of the indictments against Dorothy that helped us kill some time in a summer afternoon included:

- illegally transporting mangy dog wanted by county authorities for biting a neighborhood lady.
- flying a Kansas farm house without a valid pilot's license.
- failure to pay seer for crystal ball reading in his personal wagon
- hit-and-run incident murdering a witch having a friendly conversation with Munchkins in Munchkin Land by landing a 70-ton Kansas farm house directly on her alone.
- conspiracy to aid and abet Mr. Scarecrow's escape from

his owners.

- standing by and allowing a Munchkin extra to hang himself on the set. (Munchkin hanging was pure rumor and never happened.)
- receiving stolen goods (pair of ruby slippers) from a smiling witch named Glinda.
- cruelty to animals for slapping a hapless cowardly lion.
- conspiring with two adults (Mr. Scarecrow and Mr. Tin Man) to steal apples from apple orchard.
- resisting citizens' arrest by the flying monkeys.
- trespassing in the haunted forest, illegally entering the haunted castle, and trampling a farmer's planted poppy field.
- conspiracy and receiving goods (broom) stolen from the wicked witch.
- conspiracy in home invasion and liquidation of resident witch.
- abuse of mangy dog named Toto by failing to properly feed and water him during trip from Kansas to Oz and back.
- impersonating a 12-year-old actress.

WIWAK kids could be cruel to one another. Yet, rarely would you hear any of the four letter words that seem to have lost their shock value today. It may sound like fantasy, but kids showed plenty of respect for one another. Kids were more original back then, when telling each other to go to "H-E-double hockey sticks!" Some invectives included:

- Dry Up!   • Bug off!

- Shove off!
- Take a flying leap! Go fetch!
- Make me! Drop dead!
- Bite me!
- Beat it!
- Shove it!
- Forget about it!
- Stuff it!
- Piss off!

- Kiss off!
- Up yours!
- Get lost!
- Get outta here!
- Go fly a kite!
- Scram!
- Talk to the hand!
- Dial 411 and ask who cares!
- Blow!

WIWAK Mom was constantly trying to get us to eat something that was "good for us." Why she persisted was a mystery to us. Sometimes, Ma thought she was a master cook and tried to deceive her brood at the table by covering rejected foodstuffs with gravy or other culinary forms. Yet, we weren't falling for any of her recycled offerings. Imploring us to try it because it "tastes like chicken," we shot back, "That's what we want – chicken!" As the baby of the family, I quickly learned from my older siblings what was edible and what was to be avoided at all costs, no matter what Ma said. There were some comical descriptions for taboo food at our dinner table.

- tree branches – broccoli
- maggots – rice
- shit on a shingle – dry beef on toast
- dry steak – liver
- camouflaged dry steak – liver with gravy
- blood clots – tomato chunks in chili or spaghetti sauce

(gravy)

- seaweed with veins – spinach
- brain lobes – cauliflower
- toe jam dip – Limburger cheese
- moldy nothings – mushrooms
- grout – grits

My mother actually found humor in such conversations. Yet, none of us to this very day have ever used profane language in front of her. Mom usually went into fits of uncontrollable laughter and it made me very happy to see her laughing. There was a lot of laughter in our house at

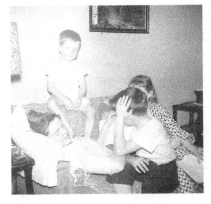

some of the silliest things. We all seemed to see humor in each other and everyday things that came into our lives. I believe it was our way of trying to forget the dire situation we were in as a family without a father.

Mrs. Tasker with three of her children- "No rest for the weary."

WIWAK there were never any television shows reflecting what went on in a house that had six kids and one bathroom. My mother, despite the lack of thousands of dollars, tried to replicate what she saw on TV and in neighbors' bathrooms. She decorated the john with knitted toilet paper covers and wallpaper featuring bucolic scenery, and placed air freshener and miniature soaps on top of the toilet. But young boys have very different and strange ideas about interior decorating. We used to sit around the dinner table and come up with laughable and outrageous ideas for the bathroom of our dreams. We always got a big kick out of seeing my mother laughing. I think that's why we came up with these goofy ideas. A few included:

- A close-up of a tearing Frankenstein gritting his teeth.
- Atom bomb mushroom exploding out of a toilet bowl.
- Skull and crossbones in a toilet
- The Titanic, Andrea Doria & Lusitania crashing into each other.
- Michelangelo's "Last Judgment" warning of "Abandon hope all ye who enter here."
- The Grim Reaper throwing up through his bony fingers
- Bela Lugosi's Dracula grimacing with teary, bloodshot eyes.
- Richard Nixon and Nikita Khrushchev debating over a toilet bowl.
- Onomatopoeia expressions plastered throughout the wallpaper – ...Pow! ...Bam! ...Snap! ...Crackle! ....Pop! etc.

WIWAK grown-ups had different sayings they used to keep their offspring in line. Some fathers would never go back and forth arguing with a child. Most dads viewed such exchanges as a waste of time and got straight to the point, especially when Mom couldn't seem to get through to them. Viewed today, some of these verbal warnings appear harsh, but it was an effective tool for most men that raised Baby Boomers. I hung around with a lot of boys and witnessed such exchanges. The men that used them got their point across quickly and never seriously assaulted any of my friends.

However, those that did defy dear old Dad were afforded the rod at times. This behavioral modification system definitely instilled respect for parents in those days. Those I heard many times were:

- Do as I say, not as I do!
- You're cruising for a bruising!
- Monkey-see, monkey-do, a good monkey can get in trouble too!
- I'll beat you into the New Year!
- After I get done with you, your mother won't recognize you!
- I'll beat you within an inch of your life!
- Stop crying or I'll give you something to cry about!
- This is gonna' hurt me more than it's gonna' hurt you!
- After I get done with you, you'll look like you've been shot at and missed and shit at and hit!
- You're getting your mouth washed out with soap!
- It's my way, or the highway!
- You sommabitch!
- I'm going to burn your ass!
- Don't pee down my back and tell me it's raining!
- I kick the stink out of kids like you just to get to a fight!
- I'm going to knock the taste out of your mouth!
- I'll knock that stupid grin off your face!
- I'll whupp you!
- Girl, your days are numbered!
- I brought you into this world, and I can take you out!

One father was contacted by police at work and asked to pick junior up at school. They told him his son skipped school to play basketball. Upon arrival at the school office, the father said to his son, "Catch this, son." The kid caught the object and saw that it was a bullet. Looking up at his dad he heard his old man say, "Skip school again and you won't catch the next one!"

WIWAK disc jockeys on the radio were as big as the musical rock and roll acts they promoted each day. Philadelphia's top 10 jocks talked 90 miles per hour and played the same 20 records all day long. They were an essential part of most teenagers' lives, and who you listened to said a lot about

The dynamic Jerry Blavat still gets the dance floors jumpin'.

you. Going to a dance where they were appearing was as big as it got for most of us living out in the sticks in Levittown. We enjoyed hearing disc jockey Jerry Blavat proclaiming with the speed of a jet that he was "the boss with the hot sauce," and the late Hy Lit stating he was the "fifth" Beatle. Kids in cars really loved late night one hour programs called "Parkology" by Blavat and others. The comedian George Carlin used many of their pitches for his stereotypical disc jockey in his nightclub act. Yet, we loved these guys and bought the albums and products that they endorsed in the Delaware Valley. Today, we even hire them as guest disc jockeys at 50th high

* Photo – from the Jerry Blavat Collection

school reunions. They are part of our life and they included:

- The Geator With the Heator (Jerry Blavat)
- Hyskie McVadio Aroonio Zoot (Hyman Lit)
- The Rockin' Bird (Joe Niagara)
- The Atomic Mouth (Joey Adams)
- Cousin Brucie (Bruce Morrow)
- Murray the K (Murray Kaufman)
- Georgie Woods – The Man With the Goods
- Frank X Feller
- Wee Willie Weber (Bill Weber)

WIWAK we didn't have many commercial snacks hanging around the house. Putting milk in soda and coating bread with sugar was a daily treat, if you were hungry. Some of these concoctions were accepted and utilized by my brothers. When we would meet with friends and relatives, challenges would inevitably arise and concoctions were prepared and eaten in front of those who doubted such culinary treats. Such times were funny beyond belief, and presented a chance to share new recipes with kids as sick as we were. The fixings we ate on a regular basis were:

- ketchup on hot dogs
- ketchup on fried eggs
- ketchup on French toast
- salt on fruit
- sugar heaped on cereal loaded with sugar
- iced coffee
- bread and bologna dipped in coffee
- cottage cheese on hamburger

- raw hamburger and salt
- toasted peanut butter sandwich with butter and mayo
- peanut butter, bacon and banana sandwiches
- onion sandwiches
- dry sandwiches
- pickle juice in a glass
- anything dealing with anchovies
- mayo on white bread
- apple butter on bread
- chow-chow on scrapple
- monkey head slop (mix leftovers from ice box and heat on stove)
- pizza pie with anything from refrigerator

WIWAK learning the value of money came quickly for most of us. Let's face it, most parents constantly told their kids that money didn't "grow on trees." On the other hand, we knew it had to grow somewhere and we wanted to get our grubby little mitts on it. There were some rich kids whose parents must have worked in nurseries with money trees, because these kids had bushels full of money all the time. But for the rest of us, there were plenty of opportunities for kids to find work as young as 12 years old. Adults in Levittown were primarily reared during the Great Depression and World War II. These adults valued hard work and were always willing to afford young kids the chance to earn money through hard work. This is something that is sorely missing today, especially considering all the large groups of kids we see hanging around day and night with nothing productive to do. Most would never entertain the idea of working in the neighborhood to get a small stack of "dead presidents" (money) for themselves. Some things we did included:

- lawn cutter and raker
- snow shoveler
- lemonade salesman
- grocery carrier
- lawn weeder
- address sign curb painter
- babysitter
- pet babysitter
- metal collector
- dog dirt remover
- soda bottle collector
- magazine salesman
- paper carrier
- G.R.I.T. salesman (America's Newspaper)
- shoeshine boy
- all-around "go for"
- car detailer
- barber shop sweeper
- window washer
- farm laborer
- boat bailer
- picnic table painter
- muskrat skinner

WIWAK no topic went uncovered in a sleepover in a tent on a humid summer night. One topic that had its grip on us and provided endless hours of entertainment was the questions and observations on the great hereafter. My best friend's dad would actually provide the clearest ideas of what it was to be dead and we would trust that he really knew all about the subject. I often thought about what my dad looked like in his final resting place after all the years that had passed. We would scare each other and wonder about the following gruesome details:

- How long did it take for skin to decay after death?
- How long did fingernails grow until they stopped?
- Did water get into the coffin when it rained?

- Could bugs get into the coffin right away?
- Could a person dig himself out if he were buried alive?
- Does the dirt above a coffin smash all coffin lids in a week or two?
- Could a person convince everyone he was dead by acting dead?
- How long did it take for a shark skin suit worn by the deceased to decay?
- Is it cold underground in a coffin?
- Do Nehru jackets worn by the dead ever decay?
- Did the funeral director stare at Marilyn Monroe's dead body?
- Would God let anyone into heaven wearing a Beehive, Ducktail or Leisure Suit?

WIWAK it seemed there was a new dance to learn almost every month. Some of the more popular dances included the following:

Peppermint Twist, Twist, Fly, Hucklebuck, Hand Jive, Hully Guly, Slop, Jerk, Cha-Cha, Mash Potatoes, Stomp, Calypso, Pony, Bunny Hop, Mouse, Mexican Hat Dance, Jitterbug, Locomotion, Limbo, Stroll, Wahtusi, Swim, and Frug.

In the early 1960's Author Mike Tasker was twisting the night away.

WIWAK - When I Was A Kid

While we were growing up in the fifties and sixties, the stores and catalogs were filled with toys that they tried to sell us. Here are some popular ones.*

- Hoola-Hoops
- Slinky
- Colorforms
- Jacks & ball
- Etch-a-Sketch
- Lincoln Logs
- Mr. Potato Head
- Pick-Up Stix
- ViewMaster & reels
- Paddle Ball
- Silly Putty
- Tipsy Tail
- Tinkertoys
- Marbles
- Cootie game
- Chatty Cathy
- Erector Set
- Matchbox Cars
- Mouse Trap game
- Toy Soldier set
- Magic Slate
- Circus Top
- Betsy Wetsy

- Clue game
- Ant Farm
- Chinese Checkers
- Play-Doh
- Crayola Crayons
- Original Barbie doll
- Original Ken doll
- Francie
- Midge
- Skipper
- Casey
- Tammy doll
- Thumbelina
- Wooly Willy
- Dark Shadows game
- Hi Heidi
- Honey West game
- Penny Brite
- Uncle Wiggily game
- Frisbee
- Krazy Ikes
- My Little Max
- Drinking Bird

- Gumby & Pokey
- Easy Bake Oven
- G.I. Joe
- Cracker Jacks surprises
- Creepy Crawlers Bugmaker
- Hands Down game
- Hopscotch
- Jump Rope
- Lite-Brite
- Old Maid card game
- Paperdolls
- Spirograph
- Tiddlywinks
- Twister
- Wagon
- Yo-yo
- Carrom Board
- Candyland game
- Chutes & Ladders
- Raggedy Ann & Andy

*www.hisforever.com/50's

Chapter 3

School Days

Mike Tasker -early 1960's
Saint Joseph the Worker
school picture.

Maureen Conroy
Mike's future wife

*"Never go to your high school reunion
pregnant or they will think that's all you have
done since you graduated."*

Erma Bombeck

When my family moved to Levittown, many schools were being built to handle the influx of children.

After they opened their doors, classes of seventy, eighty, and ninety students were not unheard of and many new schools had to have additions put on them immediately. St. Michael the Archangel School was the first Catholic grammar school in Levittown, and my brothers and sister attended. Staffed by an excellent group of nuns, they brought complete order to the overwhelming number of kids that filled their school. By the time I was eligible for school, St. Joseph the Worker School in Fallsington, Pa., was built to help handle the massive number of kids that St. Mike's was saddled with. It didn't take long before this two story, sixteen-classroom school in Fallsington experienced growing pains too; a third floor with eight more classes went up. There were kids hanging from the ceilings, yet the nuns at St. Joseph's handled classes numbering seventy or more with relative ease. The nuns, in solid partnership with parents, maintained complete control; one could hear the overhead lights hum on any given day. Each and every student had to produce in order to make the next grade, and children deemed not ready for advancement to the next grade were actually kept back. I was "selected" to stay back in sixth grade, along with twelve others boys and one girl, due to our immaturity and lackluster grades. Despite being kept back, I appreciated the fact they tried to instill in me that it was time for me to grow up and learn something. I wasn't too happy then, but I accepted my fate and learned my lesson. My mother didn't haggle with the nuns and took their decision as final. I stayed nine years in the eight-grade school. Upon graduation I attended Pennsbury High School in Fairless Hills. The classes there were large too. My school number was my social security number. I breezed through the public school and graduated with over 1500 kids in my senior class, a record number at that time.

WIWAK the normal twelve years spent in school amounted to 2,160 days, and awards were handed out for countless children who never missed one single day. School administrators needed at least two feet of snow for officials to inform local AM radio station WBCB of a one hour delay. If your principal was born in Wisconsin, forget about getting off for snow.

WIWAK our first day in first grade was a memorable and scary event for a lot of kids in Catholic schools. Leaving home was one thing, but spending a whole day in a school with someone whose face was wrapped in white like a mummy and who wore a black dress was a bit much for some six-year olds. Many children soiled their pants sitting right in their desk seats. My sister was one such offender. When the sister asked her if she had wet her dress, my sister innocently replied, "No, sister, I don't know who put water on my dress."

WIWAK the first day of school was terrifying for me, because of the gigantic toilets. I was deeply afraid of them and wouldn't use them. I managed to hold "it" in, but the school bus ride home started to shake it out of me. After I got off the bus, I only had to walk up the block to the comfort of my own commode. Sweat poured off my brow as I walked in the direction of my house. Occasional stops to make sure I was master of my bodily functions helped, but nature won out as I finally had to stop and let nature take its course.

Walking home with my legs spread apart carrying what felt like a small submarine swaying to and fro in my underwear is an experience I will never forget.

WIWAK wearing uniforms in school promoted conformity, yet we never gave it a second thought. Parents with five and six kids saved a lot of money in clothes costs.

WIWAK all the teachers commanded respect in and out of class. Teachers weren't like real people, because they didn't tolerate any nonsense like our parents did. When they told us something, we did it – bam! – no questions asked. One never, never, never – did I mention the word never – cursed within one hundred yards of their presence. How they heard anything through those starched white linens that covered their ears was something we could never figure out. Such super hearing would have made George Reeves (Superman) jealous. Even if a kid made the mistake of saying something base in their presence, adding "Pardon my French" would not stop the slap meant to knock the filth out of his/her mouth. Teachers took the place of parents--period. To actually challenge their authority was an exercise in futility. Students who gambled with them in this area attained the same results as any cartoon villain dealing with Mighty Mouse.

WIWAK there was no sickness that went through Lower Bucks County that didn't stop for a week or two in the hallowed halls of St. Joseph the Worker grammar school. The year 1959 remains seared in my mind to this day as the Year of the Big Flu. For a boy in first grade, seeing a kid running down the hallway with a hand over his mouth trying to stop nature from taking its course is a sight never quite forgotten. Sometimes a sick classmate would inadvertently spray nearby students in a feeble attempt to reach a wastebasket or the door of the classroom. Cries of "Sister, dear God, help me!" took on the urgency of soldiers calling out for a medic on the battlefield. We quickly learned that many kids didn't have a stomach for such incidents, as they hurled their breakfasts in sympathetic response. One week the influenza blitz took on comical slapstick proportions, with one sick student running to the bathroom slipping on the droppings of the sick pupil who had preceded him. Kids were falling like flies all over the building, and some left gifts for the bus drivers on the trip home. The most memorable event of this particular week occurred when one student, a kid named Jimmer, told the nun at her desk that he was sick and wanted a pass for the bathroom. Always one to adhere to the rules, the nun dutifully began to fill out the pass, but Mother Nature was in no mood to wait. Jimmer covered Sister and her desk and the pass with an adequate supply of his stomach's contents. The immolation of the teacher and her desk became part of Jimmer's legend in the school. Today, such situations would be treated as infectious biohazards, but back then being chosen by the nun to go get the mop and green sawdust at the end of the hall was an honor that most kids vied for. No matter what the weather outside, windows were opened wide and the cleanup commenced. Some kids actually headed for the bathroom, since they couldn't handle the smell of the cleaning fluids. Class clowns couldn't pass up commenting on the cleanup, as the oozing stew on the floor was mopped up in the frigid room. In the end, the nuns plowed on despite the flu bug. Curiously, they never got sick during the onslaught. As we got older and wiser, we believed these nuns never even got headaches –they just gave them!

WIWAK our desks in school were used for more than academics. Hiding beneath wooden desks was considered excellent protection for students in case of nuclear attack by the Russians. Some students and teachers believed a nuclear bomb was survivable even if it landed out in the school

1950's school children assuming the "Duck and Cover" position practicing for nuclear war.*

playground. Therefore, we practiced often diving under our safe, cozy desks whenever the emergency siren rang. These drills became common and usually drew yawns from the participants; there were no counselors for children actually terrified of such an eventuality. I really don't believe a lot of people at this time understood the devastating destruction of a nuclear blast. Sister Angelina was a prime example of someone apparently uninformed about nuclear war. We made jokes about the nun among ourselves, miles away from the school and convent. One classmate captured her mannerisms perfectly, mimicking her and saying she would probably tell us the following before a twenty megaton nuclear bomb hit: "Class, should a bomb land nearby, daily recess will probably be interrupted for a few days until things

* **From the U.S. Civil Defense Instructional Film, "Duck and Cover," starring Bert the Turtle.**

41

are cleaned up."

WIWAK teachers always demanded single file when exiting the classroom, even if it was for a nuclear drill. If we were going to be incinerated, we wanted people to find our incinerated outlines in a perfectly straight line. They'd probably say, "This line of pulverized bones has to be Sister Denise's class; she always insisted on perfectly straight lines."

WIWAK hugging a teacher was a normal ritual as kids exited the school doors and climbed on buses each afternoon. Most kids really liked the discipline the nuns expected in their classrooms. Despite all the horror stories that many Catholic school graduates talk about, most nuns were wonderful women with great personalities. They all had one thing in common – they loved children. Some of the best nuns I was fortunate to get were strict disciplinarians. I only had one teacher who was not a nun the entire time I attended grade school.

WIWAK a six foot tall, 120-pound eighth grader named Raymond made the mortal mistake of telling a four-foot, nine-inch tall nun, Sister Perpetua, to "go jump" after she had just accused him of talking during a test. Until this very day those of us who sat nearby on that 98-degree afternoon in the spring don't know if he was suffering from heat stroke or just forgot whom he was talking to when he got out of his desk, raised his fist, and took a boxer's stance. But Sister Perpetua, built like Rocky Marciano and faintly resembling him down to the hair on his arms, immediately leaped from her desk chair. Racing toward poor Ray in her high heeled granny pumps that all nuns wore then, she instantly feigned a right jab. Ray took the bait. When he tried to block it, Sister landed a bone-crushing left uppercut to Ray's chin that sent him to the tiled floor in only five seconds of the first and final round. Sister was never challenged again that year and went on to post a flyweight record of 7-0 during her career as a nun. As for Mr.Tulli, he later followed up his boxing debut to Sister by losing a slap-fest to his mother in the school parking lot. This was followed by a one second knockout registered by Pop after Mom spilled the beans at home. When he awoke, Ray's father dragged him to the convent that night to apologize. Raymond never caused a problem again. Ironically, he now teaches at-risk students and deals very well with kids who exhibit poor behavior in class. He still remembers Sister Perpetua, his Dad, and all the details of that warm spring day in class like it happened yesterday.

WIWAK the school snack of choice, at five cents each, were Philadelphia soft pretzels. These pretzels weren't wrapped in cellophane; they came fresh from the bakery in a laundry basket. Sometimes there was so much salt on the pretzels they had water condensing on them. During recess kids carried the salty treats in the pockets of their shirt and pants. The most prized part of the German inspired treat was the knot in the middle.

WIWAK a pint bottle of milk was five cents in school. Chocolate milk and orange drink were ten cents each. Both came in glass bottles and, unlike drinks in plastic cartons, had a clean taste. A week didn't go by in class that a kid didn't drop a bottle during lunch. I preferred chocolate milk along with a Philadelphia soft pretzel, for a grand total of 15 cents.

WIWAK gym equipment to play with during recess was non-existent. If you wanted to jump rope, play with a yo-yo, or play cards, you supplied it. Recess took place on the school's parking lot or roof, with few teachers supervising. School safeties patrolled the play area to ensure proper behavior and to fill in for teachers. Any violation of the rules would result in a trip to safety court on Fridays, where you would be judged and sentenced by a jury of eighth graders.

WIWAK recess was a perfect time to be inducted into the world of gambling. The most inviting game for boys to play was cards – not poker, but baseball card games. These cards included such memorable games as Closies, Flipsies, Knocksies and Topsies. Closies involved throwing cards, and the closest card to the wall won all the other cards, while Flipsies was just flipping cards to the ground, with the face side being the winner. Setting up a card against the wall and knocking it down with another card gave you the winning pot of cards in Knocksies, and Topsies was a game in which contestants tried to top another card to gain all the cards flipped. All along the back wall of the school kids tried their luck at this game of chance. Many can trace their gambling addictions back to elementary school recess. A five-cent pack of cards, with bubble gum included, helped one gain entry into the daily action that rivaled anything going on in Vegas. Great fortunes and reputations were won and lost, and taking stock of one's winnings of baseball cards was a common occurrence, as we went back to classes where nuns warned us of the sinful nature of gambling. Ironically, baseball cards were as worthless as Confederate money the following year, if you attempted to use them again in a card game. Nobody wanted last year's cards, since there was no real market for them then. So, over the summer most kids would throw away a year's worth of winnings and begin buying new cards for the upcoming gambling season beginning in September. Today, those same discarded cards are worth thousands of dollars.

WIWAK there were no televisions in school, even in the teacher's lunch room. The only pictures we saw were in books, newspapers, magazines, and slide projectors. The early slide projectors had graphics below the picture for a teacher or student to read as it progressed. New-and-improved models later had narration between beeps. We wondered aloud at the time, "What will science think of next?"

WIWAK a majority of girls had never been warned about their special entry into womanhood by their parents or teachers. Now that I think about it, there were a lot of mysteries involving sex in schools at this time. So, when pale little Mary jumped out of her desk during fifth period mathematics class screaming she was "losing blood fast between her legs," most of us, girls included, were at a complete loss as to what had caused her wound to begin with. Even after the nun rushed her out of the room, someone muttered that she was having her first period. Most of the boys, myself included, couldn't figure out how you could have your first period when it was already the fifth period of the day! Later, a wiser Mary came back to the class and everything returned to normal.

WIWAK games in school were thought up by and organized by the kids themselves. Teachers observing the organized chaos were on hand to attend those who were wounded during the games. Some game names included Fox & Geese, Jailbreak, War, Guns, and Breakout. Fox & Geese, Jailbreak and Breakout were basically various versions of tag. War and Guns usually were played in school with make believe weapons, and at home with our play handguns and rifles. If boys could compete and excel in the above exercises, anything life threw at them would be anti-climactic. Usually, by the end of the year, most of these games would be prohibited, due to mothers complaining about ripped clothing and bruised knees and elbows from some of the more energetic participants.

WIWAK eating lunch at our school involved retrieving a brown paper bag from the closet at the back of our classroom. More times than not many children would grab a brown paper bag with a round wet ring on the bottom of it, packed lovingly by their mothers four hours earlier. Refrigeration was unavailable at our school for all the lunches kids hauled in each day from home. The smells emanating from the classrooms during the noon hour were curious, to say the least. Some "rich" kids had metal lunch boxes with TV and cartoon characters embossed on them. The contents of their thermoses rarely remained cold or hot, and dropping them in class always resulted in the glass lining being shattered. Carrying a metal lunch box past sixth grade was definitely not cool, and today these same lunch pails are collector's items worth a tidy sum of money. Once again, most kids threw them away by the end of the year.

WIWAK air conditioning at school was unheard of! We didn't miss what nobody seemed to have. The movie theaters, department and food stores, and people with expensive cars had air conditioning. What got us was the nuns who never seemed to sweat, nor complain about all the layers of clothes that made up their habits.

WIWAK school doors were always opened and unguarded. There was no need for police in school buildings. Teachers provided law and order in and out of the school throughout the school calendar year. Public school buildings were enjoyed twelve months a year by kids of all academic and athletic abilities. Kids actually enjoyed summer school programs and most of my classmates, Catholic school products, were truly amazed at all the toys and crafts that public school offered during summer school. Some kids (not me) actually threw volleyballs and basketballs on the roofs of the school during summer school, then came back later to take them home.

WIWAK the "dim lights" were stuck in class with the "bright" kids. We knew instinctively that no matter how much we studied, Jane and Brendan, star pupils in our class whose last names I will leave blank, would always be the smartest. None of us would have been surprised to see either student having lunch with the teachers and discussing lesson plans and student progress reports, they were that smart. After deducing this fact of life, kids decided to compete for other more attainable positions in class life. Many slots

47

required no brains, including the following: most popular, best dancer, class clown, bully, quietest, top curser, most conceited, toughest, biggest stuck-up, prettiest, princess in residence, best drawer, skinniest, fattest, fashion plate, weirdest, moron, stool pigeon, teacher's pet, belching-talking artist, knuckle cracker, pig at lunch, all-around slob, nitwit, coolest, and class skank. Were these posts really coveted? Maybe not. But quite a few kids filled the spots by default.

WIWAK fighting in grammar school was unusual. In high school it usually took place off school grounds. Grammar school fights usually saw combatants vowing to "kill" one another. If all the boys who ever threatened to kill a fellow student were arrested back then, my class would have been mostly all female students. When tempers cooled, more often than not, another classmate would intervene and tell both kids to shake hands and "forget about it!" I believe most kids in my school were just afraid to fight, but had to play the part in front of their peers. I know I did on several occasions.

WIWAK lunch was one complete hour. This allowed students who lived close enough to walk home and eat lunch with their mothers, and it enabled those left behind at school to play and talk with their classmates for an extended period of time. Children went out to recess in all kinds of weather, and no disease could keep us inside. If we were coming off brain surgery, the good nuns would arrange for a portable gurney to wheel us outside into the parking lot. They would remind us that besides water, fresh air was free and good for us. Girls played with girls and boys played with boys, and most kids in our school were physically fit.

WIWAK the Pledge of Allegiance was recited each day before prayers. On special occasions we sang God Bless America. Everyone stood in class and lawsuits by parents were unheard of.

WIWAK we had the same teacher all year long.

WIWAK soda was not allowed in schools. Water was available at each end of the school hallways and was not viewed as some caustic fluid to be avoided at all costs. There were two days when teachers let us have candy in school – Halloween and St. Valentine's Day. Valentine's Day was the one day kids with raging hormones had a chance to tell each other they "liked" them. Students would put cards in a pile and the nun would hand them out to the name listed on the envelope. I would write all kinds of sweet gushy things to the girl I liked that week, but never signed my name.

WIWAK girls who "developed" early in schools usually hid the incriminating evidence by holding books at chest level in the hallways.

WIWAK nothing broke up a class more than passing wind. Usually a boy that expended gas ran a big risk of getting caught by Sister. The excuse, "better out than in," was no excuse as far as the nuns were concerned. The nun also had air spray on hand for those who couldn't control themselves.

WIWAK class size was not an issue with the educational establishment, especially in Catholic schools. In my first grade class there were 73 kids. We thought we had it good since classes at another grammar school nearby had 98 children. The biggest technological item in my first grade class was a colored Abacus. Not only did the sisters control the class, students learned to read, write, add and become functioning American citizens.

WIWAK yelling the word "snow" for the first time on a cold winter day always brought the entire class, including the teacher, to the classroom windows in November. By March nobody moved. The only snow we were looking forward to by that time was a 10 cent snow cone with flavored syrup on it.

WIWAK some of the best laughs among my buddies came in the church, which was attached to the school itself. Most kids knew that church was meant for prayers and meditation. Yet, class clowns saw this as a great opportunity to try out new routines. Suppressing laughs and smiles from observant nuns was crucial to avoiding corporal punishment – translation – getting your face smacked raw. Some kids would intentionally try to get friends to laugh, so that they could laugh when Sister So-And-So dispensed justice to the offender.

WIWAK putting your arm around a male friend's neck and walking around during recess at school, or down a neighborhood street, was not construed as deviant behavior. It was an overt statement of being best buddies, and frankly it felt good to be a close buddy with certain classmates. Sometimes I would be entangled with two other boys I knew, and we never, ever gave it a second thought. We were and still are buddies for life to this day.

WIWAK our teachers demanded we write with a pen with an ink cartridge in it. I don't really know why the nuns preferred an ink pen to a ballpoint pen. Most of the guys in class said that the school must have had a piece of the action in ink cartridge companies. I do know that nuns insisted on order and cleanliness in all things and gave out marking period grades for these practices. Ink pens provided a distinct marking when applied to paper, and we always wrote Jesus, Mary & Joseph at the top of each page in our composition books with these pens. Using a ball point pen would get a kid's hands slapped with a ruler. However, there was one advantage; the ink cartridge was the perfect instrument for splashing a classmate's shirt with, especially when he/she wasn't looking. Many a mother made a trip to the principal's office to complain about expensive shirts and uniforms being splotched with ink. 'Ink versus Ballpoint' was just another mystery of the universe that was never fully explained to us.

WIWAK pleasing the teacher in class was a primary focus of most students. There was fierce competition to get called on by the teacher. Classrooms in the school resembled some frenetic version of Jeopardy each time a nun asked a question of the class. Before the nun was done with her question, most kids had their hands waving in the air with the answer. There was no calling out answers, because that would be an infraction subject to extreme disciplinary action. Fifty, sixty kids exploded in their chairs, some holding onto their desks, stretching to get closer to the questioner, yelling out "Ster!" because saying "Sister" took too long. Anything to get called on was the name of the game. If the nun's selection happened to give the wrong answer, the class exploded again as the last syllable fell out of the errant student's lips. One twist to waving one's hand and stretching out of the desk was to feign a pained expression on one's face while yelping, "Ster!" Such expressions let Sister know that you might die right there in class if she failed to call on you.

WIWAK a nice shirt, slacks, tie and shoes were formal attire for most Baby Boomers in school. Unkept students were few and far between and usually picked up cruel nicknames like Gomez, Pugsley, Cousin It, Goober, and Gomer, the names of nerdy or weird TV characters. Furthermore, shoes were normally worn for church and school only, sneakers or bare feet being the rule at other times. Of course, we NEVER wore sneakers to school! Taking care of school shoes and wearing them for one full school year was standard practice for most kids. Getting them resoled in a place called a "Shoe Repair Shop" was also standard procedure. My brother's first job when he was 13-years old was at the shoe shop, earning a whole 50 cents an hour. He made good tips from patrons and he fixed my shoes and taught me how to give shoes a proper military shine, which I use to this day.

WIWAK the only thing safe to leave at school was a book. Anything else was gone. It didn't matter if the school was a religious one or not, because thieves come in all shapes, sizes, and religions.

WIWAK walking on the back of the shoe of the person walking in front of you was a game we constantly played on each other in school. Seeing a kid stumble in a school line kept us laughing. Some kids had to buy new shoes months before they should have due to the games we played on each other.

WIWAK smoking on the bus was something older teens did every day – but always in the back of the bus, since it was against the rules. Bus drivers in those days didn't seem to care too much about such infractions, since most of them carried Camels or Winstons in their shirt pockets. The kids who broke the rules told us they could quit smoking any time they wanted to, but they didn't want to. These were the same kids who five years later in 1968 told us that marijuana would be "legal in five years." Today, they still smoke, but now at $10 per pack, and Mary Jane is still illegal in most states.

WIWAK schools in our area were named after saints and prominent adults. There were no schools like P.S. 25. Some names included Walt Disney, Albert Schweitzer, Neil Armstrong, Eleanor Roosevelt, Carl Sandburg, Truman, JFK, St. John Neumann, St. Joseph, Immaculate Conception, and St. Michael the Archangel. Many of the luminaries, minus the saints, attended the school dedications in Levittown in the 1950s.

WIWAK public and private schools were never called off because it was too hot. Once the thermometer hit the high 90s, nuns in private schools would allow us to unbutton our top dress shirt buttons and loosen our ties. This was sometimes followed by allowing students a trip to the end of the hall to get three seconds of "free" water from the communal water fountain. This was not an easy move with seventy-three kids in a class, and water faucet monitors were given the job of letting each kid have three seconds of water. Usually, the child selected to dispense the water was bribe-proof, not one of the gang. Some slobs would put their whole mouths over the fountain hole, and nobody wanted to follow them, but water with a few germs was better than nothing. Amazingly, not too many kids got sick during the spring months. The nuns were amazing in their full habits. We never saw them sweat.

WIWAK school was never called off because it was too cold. We all learned very early in life that cold weather usually happened in winter, and we learned to live with it. Television didn't cover an impending cold front as if it was the end of the world. In fact, weathermen just gave viewers the cold facts, nothing more, nothing less. Our solution to extreme weather was plenty of clothes in layers and a substantial breakfast prepared by mom. Then, out we trudged to school. Parents reminded us that cold weather was good for us. Some even said it would "blow the stink off" us!

WIWAK the first Spanish-speaking kid in school was bombarded with questions from the other boys, who wanted to learn dirty words in Spanish. Despite having had children transfer in from Germany, France, Scotland, and the Netherlands, not once did any of the guys express a wish to learn how to curse in those languages. I thought that was odd. One particular item they also wanted to find out about was the strange powers of the Spanish Fly from our new amigo. This was a drug that supposedly made a girl want to go all the way. This was odd behavior from Catholic school boys who should have known such tactics were a mortal sin.

WIWAK it was the curse of all curses to follow a brother or sister that was outstanding in school, and then get their old teachers. Following a legacy could be tough, and teachers didn't let the younger sibling forget the standard his brother or sister set. There's something to be said for walking into class an unknown commodity.

WIWAK spring was yo-yo time in schools. As soon as the winter snows began disappearing, yo-yos of all shapes and sizes appeared on the school playground. Some kids had trouble making the yo-yo go up and down, while others showed off their stuff with some of the following yo-yo tricks: walking the dog, over the waterfall, shotgun, around the world, rock the cradle, spaghetti, and skin the cat. Weeks of yo-yo play would go by before kids tired of the game.

WIWAK the sisters drilled into us knowledge of the Holy Ghost, but nobody remembers when the Holy Ghost was replaced by the Holy Spirit. Why they made the name change remains a mystery in itself. However, baseball announcer Phil Rizzuto's Holy Cow and Daily Planet editor Perry White's Great Caesar's Ghost remained unchanged.

WIWAK teachers in both private and public schools didn't take any silly nonsense. Children actually got expelled from schools to maintain order within the student body. Most students actually learned something about polite manners, which would later help them in life.

WIWAK we ate lunch every day at our desks because the cafeteria had been converted into classes due to the influx of students. Some moms had to be creative on meatless Fridays packing lunches. Nobody would dare eat meat on Fridays in front of the nuns.

WIWAK classmates learned very early in school that bribes could be utilized to get friends in class in trouble with the nuns. If a student was doodling, some kids would offer a baseball card to another kid to get him to tell on the offender. A bribe offering Hank Aaron's card would always get some kid to squeal. After the payoff, they would watch the fireworks begin. Sister wasted no time thrashing the budding artist in front of everyone. All art was kept for evidence to be shown later in the day to two other enforcers – his/her parents.

WIWAK teachers collected money weekly from some of the students for their passbook savings accounts. Although, every kid I hung around with found it hard to imagine having any money each week for sister. My biggest problem was trying to dredge up an extra nickel for a Philadelphia soft pretzel in school. These passbook misers probably had quite a stash waiting for them by the late '60s and early '70s.

WIWAK the worst feeling in the world was going to school on Monday and hoping the nun wouldn't discover you didn't do your homework. I learned quickly that there was a price to be paid for not doing homework. Talking in class was just as bad. It was a daily ritual for me getting caught without my work, or talking in class, and having to walk three miles home from school at the young age of eight after a one hour detention.

WIWAK some high school teachers smoked in front of kids to drive them crazy. Many private school teachers knew that many of their students smoked, and they would light up right in class in front of them. Today this would be viewed as a poor example, but in the late '50s and early '60s certain teachers got away with this behavior. Non-smoking kids in class thought it was funny that the teacher was torturing the smokers.

WIWAK my dear old mother told the nuns to put my "head through the wall" if I gave them any trouble at all. I never did!

Chapter 4

Boy Talk

Best Buds - Bobby Murray, Jimmy Karcher,
dog Theodore and Mike Tasker

"Once a man, twice a boy."
Shakespeare, taken from Hamlet
(Often quoted by Katherine Conroy-Mike's Mother-In-Law)

WIWAK a recurring topic of conversation among the guys was an attempt to understand why most holidays and occasions had the word "happy" in front of them, except Christmas, which had "merry." Our conversations were not the most intellectually based dialogues.

WIWAK boys would sit around and talk about how they

would eventually "get" a girlfriend. With hormones clouding any rational thought, mine included, we talked about how our wives would have to cook and clean for us. As pre-teens we weren't looking for soul mates, but objects that would cook for us. Girls with any brains or opinions need not apply. A few of the guys from the old gang got their wish with some hot tomatoes, but most of them were divorced in short order. One close friend didn't make it three weeks. I'm sure his wife didn't appreciate his ideas about marriage.

WIWAK there was an occasional tragic death in the community involving a teenager. Of course, there were always those boys that "knew" the deceased. These braggarts usually told us they would have been killed too, but at the last moment canceled getting together with the kid that died. If all the boys who stretched the truth on their brush with death were actually assembled, a Greyhound bus would have been needed on the night the death actually occurred.

WIWAK most girls in the neighborhood, when they did talk to me and my friends, said they wanted to become nurses so they could work with Dr. Kildaire and Dr. Ben Casey, two famous television personalities. Not one female ever mentioned wanting to meet the very capable television doctor, Dr. Zorba, a septuagenarian!

WIWAK there were no families in Levittown who were people of color. Racial discrimination was still a big problem in America, and our parents' generation still had not dealt with it. As young kids we didn't know that a problem of civil rights even existed in good old Levittown, and we never talked about it. If something was out of sight it was also out of mind.

WIWAK many of us feared an array of spooks, goblins, and things that went bump in the night. However, there was one dreaded monster most kids would all agree on: the friendly neighborhood dentist. Dracula, Godzilla, King Kong, Martians, the Jersey Devil, and Midnight Mary could not conjure up the level of horror that came to the surface when kids walked into a dentist's in the 50's. The smell of the building, office furniture that hadn't changed since 1910, and the dreaded sound of drilling in the next room paralyzed us with terror. Kids knew that when they entered that next room they would exit with cotton and blood in their mouths, and severe pain from a doctor who should have been drilling coal in a mine. It's no exaggeration when a Baby Boomer says smoke and sparks flew when dentists drilled teeth in those Wonder Years.

WIWAK nothing hurt more than being called a "pansy" by another boy in the neighborhood. The kid who proclaimed, "Sticks and stones will break my bones, but names will never hurt me" probably was never called a pansy.

WIWAK we used to like to irritate one another by repeating what someone just said. Of course, some nitwits carried the game too far and a bitter argument ensued. One way to end the game was to say the copycat was a jerk, and he couldn't repeat that about himself.

WIWAK we couldn't stop talking about Bela Lugosi when it was learned that he was buried in his Dracula outfit. Nobody has really topped Bella as the infamous count.

WIWAK resolving what to do with the frozen corpse of

WIWAK - When I Was A Kid

Walt Disney in the future was an issue we could never seem to come to a consensus on. (We believed at the time that his body was frozen for future resurrection by science, but Disney apparently was cremated two days after his death and his ashes were placed in Forest Glen Cemetery, California).

WIWAK speaking in rhymes showed how "cool" we were when we were engaged in conversation. It was early rapping without sound effects. One ditty I used to use all the time went, "I'm the man of the band. Don't give me any lip, potato chip. Understood, Robin Hood? You know what I mean, Jellybean? I don't smoke, joke, take dope, drink Coke, but I do play! Enough said, Ted." What's it all mean? I didn't know then, or now!

WIWAK conversation about someone's dad usually began with the words, "My old man..." I couldn't understand fully why some boys would show disrespect for their fathers.

WIWAK a neighborhood boy whose mother never bothered to wipe his nose or tell him how to maintain proper personal hygiene always seemed to have goo hanging beneath his nose from the first frost until springtime. Needless to say, this youngster didn't have many friends to talk with.

Chapter 5

Scary Stories

**1950's neighborhood children playing
Cowboys and Indians***

'Death is not a period, but a comma."
Amos Traver (favorite quote of M.E. Tasker)

WIWAK we got real live dyed chicks for Easter. One year we managed to successfully keep five Easter chicks alive (Pinky, Pudgy, Killer, Chick and Alfalfa) well into the summer. Gone on the birds were the green, purple, blue, pink and orange dyed fluff which had helped us identify them. As they grew older we started to lose interest, while mom started to gain interest in making our formerly cute chicks Saturday night supper. Mom, who was raised

***Photo from The Mount Carmel Academy -
Archdiocese of New Orleans.**

in the city, had no expertise in butchering live birds, but a neighbor with a farming background volunteered to chop off their heads and pluck their feathers. This proved to be a traumatic experience for us. Watching our old feathered buddies streaking around our back yard headless was quite a shock. After the chickens had stopped dancing around, our neighbor proceeded to pluck and gut our ex-buddies. Mouths agape, we knew instinctively that this would be a day in Tasker family history that we would never forget. Needless to say, none of us could bring ourselves to eat what we used to love and play with. My mother had no problem eating her portion of chicken that night. Looking around the table at the long faces, mom started laughing uncontrollably and eventually composed herself long enough to tell us, "Come on, eat up! It tastes just like chicken."

WIWAK many of us vacationed at the New Jersey shore, renting a house for a week and coming back year after year. Atlantic City, Wildwood, Cape May, Point Pleasant, Seaside Heights, and Ocean City - we were as familiar with identifying family vacation retreats as we were with identifying passing automobiles. One place that no family vacationed in, however, was the mysterious little town of Brigantine, New Jersey. Brigantine, adjacent to world famous Atlantic City, was home to the infamous green head fly. Numbering in the billions, the green head fly could bring the hardiest outdoorsman to his knees in literally a matter of moments. It was the one town in all of New Jersey that even the Jersey Devil avoided. But yet unaware of the pint sized monster, one year our family decided to take a day trip to Brigantine.

In the car on the way down my brother's friend, Billy, warned us that he'd heard the Jersey Devil tried to take up residence there immediately following World War II, but the "greenie" kicked his forked tail out of there. Even white sharks avoided this tiny blood thirsty winged predator by bypassing its shores, he warned. Thinking our brother's friend had a vivid imagination, we equated him with one of those old bearded men in the horror flicks who warned folks to beware of the doom that was right around the corner. We listened intently to Billy's yarn instead of observing women walking down the streets of Brigantine with newspaper wrapped around their legs. Motoring through the town we also failed to note that almost every shore bungalow had a screened-in porch and there was no boardwalk. As soon as we parked, we reached for our towels and raced to see who could hit the surf first. Throwing the towels in a pile we ran to the water's edge. I was the youngest and last in as usual, and I tried to body surf the huge waves hitting the beach that day. While we waited for the perfect wave, the flies started landing on the fresh meat from Levittown. At first we just slapped the flies away and concentrated on having fun. But, the greenies had sounded the alarm and literally hundreds of hungry winged warriors zeroed in on us. Literally in a matter of minutes the airspace around us took on a greenish hue and flies began feasting on our white flesh. These critters even knew how to hold their breath for a long time as we attempted to submerge under the surf to get them to let go of us. For the flies the saltwater added spice to our flesh and they continued to chomp away. We knew at that very instant that we were outgunned and out of our league against these little green vampires. It only took seconds for my bloodied and swollen brothers, sister, friend and mother to grab our fly covered towels on the beach and race toward the old jalopy. With our dignity in shreds we took refuge in the car and the flies covered the windows looking for ways to get inside. With lumpy and swollen skin, we headed to a cedar lake 30 miles from the scene of the crime. Even though we emerged from the lake with brown skin, we didn't have to fight anymore insects. Nothing compares to the horror of Brigantine.

WIWAK swimming in the community pool could be a dangerous undertaking when literally 700 people were in it at the same time. Getting bombed by a flying five-year-old near the edge of the pool was commonplace, if you chose to swim underwater. On some days it was so crowded that you couldn't swim at all. However, we felt fortunate to escape the 90-plus degree heat in 95 degree water. Unfortunately, some kids mistook the pool for a toilet. To compensate, pool directors poured copious amounts of chlorine into the pool. We could literally smell it from the parking lot. Though the pool afforded relief for the rest of our bodies, our eyes were blurred from chlorine all summer whenever we looked at street lights and television.

WIWAK swimming in a public pool naked was not viewed with the alarm that it is today. It was not unusual, nor against the law to have kids swim naked in pools. A local public school would open its indoor pool to kids aged seven to 10 years old. Most of these kids had no swim trunks, or a safe place to swim during the summer months. Hygiene not being what it is today, pool officials required all boys to bathe before swimming. After bathing, kids scampered off to swim in the spacious indoor pool. There were not just a handful of youngsters doing the backstroke and the doggie paddle, but a pool filled with screaming kids. Children were actually turned away by a man at the door when the pool reached capacity. Girls swam on different days of the week under the same rules. The only catch for them was they had to wear bathing suit caps. For Baby Boomers, this program was a god-send that pool directors called "Peanut Pooling."

WIWAK mosquitoes, or any other bug for that matter, presented little problem for the residents of Levittown, Pa.Town officials knew how to kill pests in those days with a nifty little pesticide called DDT. Viewed as a modern miracle, DDT could solve any insect problem in the newly built burbs. Ranking right behind the ice cream man, the bug spray man was the most awaited visitor to our block

DDT Spraying Truck*

each summer, especially during wet summers. Once he rolled down the street dispensing his volatile fog across well manicured lawns, an alarm was sent out to every kid. Chasing the spray truck around the development on our Schwinn bicycles was a favorite game. Strangely, I can still taste that sweet aromatic bug stew to this day. How many kids remain who saddled up on their bikes to accompany the bug man

***Photo from David Laambert -"Our Dance in the DDT," southernersjournal.com**

throughout the sections 50-plus years ago? Rachael Carson, author of Silent Spring, a documentary on DDT's damage to wildlife, ruined the good times and bug spraying ended in the mid sixties. Bug colonies that were once crushed by the bug spray man now rule the sections today, however, some good has come from my exposure to the toxic green fog. I save on my electric bill, because my skin glows in the dark. I also save on bug spray, because all I have to do to stop the pests in their tracks is to spit on them; they curl up and die like slugs getting doused with salt.

WIWAK many of the people my family knew were in the service sector. One, a cashier at a food market, said most people who worked in food stores despised the "Milk & Bread Brigade," those who flood the supermarket at the first hint of an impending snow, scrambling for bread, milk, shovels, and salt. "If weathermen said people would need sardines and prunes," she continued, "there would be a run on those, too." The more affluent people among the Milk & Bread Brigades, those who panicked with a storm was usually completely cleared the day after, were the same pessimists who rushed to build nuclear bomb shelters beneath their homes. My friend's father fit the Milk & Bread Brigade stereotype. He had a bomb shelter stocked to the gills. He was sure the Apocalypse was right around the corner, but oddly never told any of his son's friends to come to his house should the Commies start lobbing thermo nuclear bombs on Levittown. My guess then was he probably only had enough powdered milk and flour for his family, to hold them over until they surfaced into a nuclear winter; after the rest of us had been vaporized.

WIWAK critters didn't have a fighting chance in my neighborhood. Kids looked at wild animals and bugs such as snakes, crickets, moths and rodents as vermin that needed to be liquidated in one way or another. Some sick kids would trap flying insects in jars with gasoline on the bottom. Other malcontents would stage fights in a bottle between insects that were natural enemies. And then there were kids who would scald whole populations of insects with hot water from a faucet. One kid actually put a circle of fire around spiders to see if they would try to scamper through the blaze. We thought all of these tortures were good summertime entertainment.

WIWAK my grandmother lived near an air base in Horsham, Pa., which we would visit quite often during the summer. Having five uncles who fought in World War II, I heard first-hand reports from the war. Conversations among the brothers scrutinized the decisions of FDR and Eisenhower, and analyzed the course of the war in all the different theaters of conflict. It just so happened that one Sunday in the middle of such a conversation, a jet pilot flew at treetop level over us on Avenue A, crashing directly into a Bargain City Department Store. Without a word, all five jumped up and raced down the avenue, climbed the building, and attempted to save the pilot from the flaming wreckage. Failing that, my uncles pulled several shoppers to safety. One of my uncles, Jim, kept trying to save the pilot, and had to be coaxed off the roof by police and fire officials. I had never seen a grown man cry until I saw my uncle sobbing at his failed attempt to rescue the Navy pilot. These men were heroes. None of them ever boasted about their efforts in the tragedy.

WIWAK none of us ever saw anyone lose an eye, regardless of the warning of our overly cautious mothers. We saw a lot of broken bones, cuts, and scrapes of all kinds, but never an eye falling on the pavement. The two top injuries I witnessed involved knitting needles and a baseball bat. The knitting needle incident involved two kids swashbuckling with one another; when one pirate parried, the other forgot to get out of the way. The result was a knitting needle right through his hand. The other involved three girls playing softball. The catcher, crouched too close to the batter, took a shot to the skull. It's unnerving to see a girl running down the street with a bloody bat in her hand screaming, "I've killed my girlfriend!"

WIWAK Spiderman had nothing on us. Standing between two houses and wedging upward with hands and feet was a pastime we also turned into a contest. Some kids could climb higher than others without a net of any kind. My two older brothers had a leg up on the competition because this was a normal activity in the city where we came from.

WIWAK there was no such thing as privacy in a house of seven people. The only place of solitude for about seven minutes was the bathroom; even then my brothers would pick the lock and open the door and laugh when they caught me on the toilet reading a comic book.

WIWAK movies were so scary that I would not go to bed unless the lights in my room upstairs were on, but the light switch was located at the bottom of the stairs, and my older brothers would turn it off once in a while for laughs. These same movies, which caused me untold horror, are laughed at today by my son and my nephews.

Chapter 6

The Price of Things

The Rancher

A NEW HOUSE IN LEVITTOWN

•

SPECIAL INTRODUCTORY PRICE—
$8,990

$57 A MONTH!

No cash required from veterans!

From the original brochure introducing the new Levittown Homes

"Buy land. They ain't making any more of the stuff."

Will Rogers

WIWAK candy bars were only a nickel at stores everywhere.

WIWAK Kool Aid was five cents a packet. The only drawback to the instant drink was you needed at least a cup of sugar to make it drinkable.

WIWAK a summer ritual for most neighborhood entrepreneurs was the lemonade stand. Foot traffic by the old stand in the heat of August was slow. However, you could

71

always count on the friendly mailman, or a delivery man to buy a glass of fresh squeezed lemons, sugar and water. We charged two cents a cup.

WIWAK most everything we drank came in glass bottles. Any kid who could drink a 10-cent bottle of Coca-Cola was looked up to in the neighborhood. It took the powers of Superman to "swig" down the ice cold soda out of that little green bottle without letting it shoot out your nostrils. Shaking a bottle of Coke was akin to holding a loaded weapon. Soda at this time had pure cane sugar in it and not corn syrup. Translation – great taste plus the original recipe! Corn syrup changes the whole chemistry of the soda. It was not unusual to be in a grocery store, or at home, and witnessing caps and bottles exploding into the air. The constant shaking of the bottles by a truck on the way to the store, and hot temperatures would sometimes cause them to literally explode.

WIWAK flattop haircuts were one of the most popular haircuts. Cuts could be had for $1 and some barbers would even massage your neck with an electric massager.

WIWAK purchasing cigar-shaped chewing gum for five cents was an essential prop to impersonate Edward G. Robinson or Groucho Marx. It all depended on the kid buying the stogie if the Robinson routine was funny or not. Saying his famous line from his breakout movie Little Caesar -- "Is this the end of Rico?" --wasn't funny without the cigar hanging out of the mouth.

WIWAK cars could be bought new for under $2,000. New models out of Detroit were eagerly awaited by everyone, even among those of us trying to scrape up cash for our next

Pepsi Cola. Cars were not just metal and bolts, but prized new members of those nuclear families who could afford them. Songs were put out about many of these cars. Many auto companies sponsored our favorite television shows, so stars became identified with them. Kids gobbled up magazines and read everything they could about Detroit's latest offerings. Car model kits gave kids countless hours of fun putting together their dream wheels.

WIWAK new sneakers had magical powers to them. We swore new sneaks made us run faster than the old ones. Sneaks went for under $2. Durability was the key factor for moms buying new sneaks, usually Keds. Converse sneaks hovered near the $10 plateau and were out of the reach of most parents who had five kids on average, but we truly believed new sneaks had magical powers. I still swear my Keds did in fact make me jump higher! If I'd had Converse, I bet I could have jumped over the backstop fencing on a Little League baseball field.

WIWAK dogs and cats cost nothing to upkeep since most people gave them scraps right off the dinner table. Canned dog food was a rare treat and usually resembled a brown gelatinous gob that had to be sliced up in Fido's dish.

1950's metal roller skate with key for size adjustments.

WIWAK only rich kids had roller skates that were shoe and skate combined. The majority of kids had a key given that helped them

73

attach skates beneath their shoe soles. Wearing heavy metal skates each Sunday at "Roller-Rama" gave us an idea of what it was like to have leg braces.

WIWAK we didn't have to buy milk or bread for months after we moved into Levittown. Salesmen would continually leave their wares on our doorstep for us to try – competition was really fierce. The best freebie was the milk in the cool months. Sold in thick glass containers and non-homogenized, the cream would always rise to the top. Those who didn't like the cream would have to shake the bottle before swigging away. Milkmen delivered white milk, chocolate milk, and orange juice, but customers could also buy various types of bread and donuts off the bread delivery man's truck.

WIWAK gasoline companies competed for our parents' dollars by offering the best service they could provide. Yes, S-E-R-V-I-C-E! Besides pumping the 26-cents-per-gallon gasoline, service attendants would actually clean our windows and check our oil and water. Inside the station attached to the bay was a little office with vending machines that would sell 12-ounce soda for 10 cents or a pack of cigarettes for 28 cents. Upon completion of the sale, stations would give us coupons good for various promotions and it didn't stop there. Before leaving they would actually smile and thank us for our patronage. Some station operators also reminded us to "Come again." Was it all a dream?

WIWAK parents were constantly telling us to "go fly a kite" just days into the summer vacation. To combat the growing boredom, we took them up on their suggestion. Some of us forked out 25 cents and put the inexpensive paper kites together ourselves, but other kids had fathers who built their kites from scratch, creating a kite like no other. Then we'd head off to where no wires loomed overhead. Those kids who wouldn't walk to the fields inevitably wound up having their kites wrapped around overhead wires. But the rest of us had hours of fun, competing to see who could get his kite higher, until the kites resembled small specks in the wild blue yonder.

WIWAK suckers, taffys, and lollipops in one form or another were always hanging out of our mouths. The huge nickel confections could last for close to an hour before they melted away, although some kids bit them not long after putting them into their mouths. Dipping suckers in glasses of water was practiced by some kids because it changed the taste somewhat. Some mothers even made Kool Aid and froze them in the ice box in a tray with a stick, while others covered bananas with chocolate and stuck them with a stick.

WIWAK the best comic books (Marvel) cost only 10 cents.

WIWAK Christmas trees cost $2. Late Christmas Eve they were reduced to $1.

WIWAK a whole pizza pie cost $1.25, which is less than one slice today.

WIWAK Topps five-cent baseball cards were valued for their stiff piece of gum, and we loved the aroma they left on our cards as well.

WIWAK my mama pushed me around in a shopping cart and kept me quiet with a five-cent box of Animal Crackers, or a Jewish pickle. I stopped going to the store when I began to run into girls from my class at school.

WIWAK penny chewing gum offered a comic story, a fortune, and valuable gifts one could get by saving up gum wrappers.

WIWAK highways and byways were not littered with discarded bottles. Youngsters always looking to make a fast buck would scour the streets looking for soda and beer bottles. Twelve ounce bottles would fetch two cents each, while quart bottles pulled in a whole nickel.

WIWAK the going rate for getting a good report card was normally about $1 from aunts, uncles and special friends. A bad report card was sometimes not shown at home, until parents finally became suspicious. Some of these kids even tried to forge their parents' names before giving them back to Sister. Our report cards were usually handed out by the priests in the parish in front of the class. Watching kids being grilled by the priest for a poor report card was great entertainment as they squirmed and tried to explain away poor performance. Deep down inside we knew the nun was eating up some kids getting blasted by the priest.

WIWAK attending plays like "Hello Dolly" with Dorothy Lamour at the Lambertville Music Circus in New Jersey inspired quite a few of us to become thespians. Most patrons could afford the tickets without having to put it on a charge account.

WIWAK eating at McDonald's was an inexpensive proposition. For less than 50 cents we could get a cheeseburger, French fries and a coke.

WIWAK $2 would get you eight gallons of gas to fly

around town on.

WIWAK 50 cents would get you into a dance where you might see a current nationally known rock and roll singer belting out his/her most recent hit right on stage. Some stars lip synched to the hit records so they could visit more dances for personal appearances on a Saturday night.

WIWAK seeing pro-teams in any of the three major sports (baseball, football and basketball) cost less than $5 a ticket. Some basketball games were doubleheaders where you could see the Boston Celtics featuring Bill Russell playing one team, and the Philadelphia Warriors behind Wilt Chamberlain playing another squad. Parking for these events was free. In the off-season we could see some pro athletes working in city neighborhoods just like real people. Some of them worked regular jobs in food stores, car dealerships and beer distributors.

WIWAK the first ethnic food introduced to me by a close friend was an Italian hot dog. Up until then, I thought a hot dog was a hot dog, which usually cost 10 cents. Inhaling a frank with potatoes, onions, peppers and mustard atop an Italian roll was wonderful, but cost a mind boggling 75 cents.

WIWAK "canteen" was what we called a dance in our area, and it was usually held at a public elementary school. During the hot summers, it was usually moved outside to the school parking lot. Admission was a hefty 25 cents.

WIWAK our public pools (Levittown Public Recreation Association) had six different locations to cool off thousands of people each year for the annual family membership fee of

$6. The pools were packed all summer and they featured both a high diving board and a low diving board. A pool tag enabled members to visit any LPRA pool. Boomers of all ages,

L.P.R.A. pool in early Levittown, Pa. Bathing caps were mandatory for women and girls.

shapes, and sizes lined up by the hundreds to jump, jack-knife, cannon ball, flip, back-flip, and watermelon off the diving boards into the packed pools. Some kids even worked on their acting by faking heart attacks and taking a shot to the midsection before falling into the chlorine blue water far below. We were not allowed to jump off the boards until the previous swimmer reached the side of the pool. Sometimes the line would be so long that the would-be diver would be dry before getting his chance to do his best version of Tarzan leaping off a jungle cliff. Each pool had a building that housed bathrooms, concession stands, a lifeguard station, and a second floor sundeck. Outside the building there was also a basketball court closed in by a metal fence. By the time I was old enough to venture up to the second floor, it was off limits due to cracking wood. Fifty years later when they tore the pool building down, a man who had dropped his class ring as he set it on the cinderblock wall atop the deck in the 1950's had it recovered and returned to him.

WIWAK we swam so much at the pool that it took until

early October to finally get rid of swimmer's ear. Some kids who tanned easily didn't lose their bronze look until late September. Our pool tags attached to our bathing suit turned white by the end of the summer. I often wonder what permanent effect all that chlorine had on our bodies and eyes.

WIWAK an enterprising man came around the sections selling snow cones, candy, and cigarettes each summer. He converted a Volkswagen bus and honked on his horn to alert everyone he was in the neighborhood. If someone got a snow cone with a star on the cup, the lucky recipient was not charged the usual 10 cents for the frosty treat. The entrepreneur's real name was Emmanuel, but we just called him Snowee, or beep.

WIWAK the ice cream man came around a few times each day once the weather began to get warm. Swarms of kids would line up for their favorite flavors.

WIWAK cutting the lawn was done with a push mower. Small

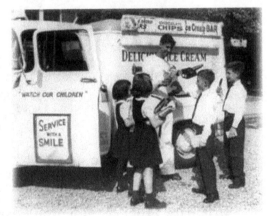

Children buying ice cream from the ice cream man- 1964.*

hand shears were used to trim around bushes and spots that couldn't be reached with the mower. Cutting lawns earned young entrepreneurs $1 for a small lawn, and $2 for a big lawn.

* Photo courtesy of Joe Marazzo-
www.deliciousicecream.com

Chapter 7

Levittown

Cowgirl Jane Alexander and Cowboy Bob Cotter played with two friends on a summer's day in 1956 in Levittown, N.Y. Bob wrote, "All the kids were great, we were originals, products of a grand experiment that did not go awry."*

"I always thought of Levittown as a joke."
Bill Griffith

WIWAK the Levittown communities, in Pennsylvania, New Jersey, and New York, were

*Website-Early Levittown and Beyond by Frank Barning and Friends

probably among the most unique housing developments in America following World War II. Why? Like a good Twilight Zone TV episode, there were no old people in Levittown – it was wall-to-wall young families that dominated the landscapes. Overwhelmingly, it was a youth culture with those that settled in the community. Kids filled each street where 17,500 houses popped up out of prime Bucks County farmland. Everything, I mean everything, was new – schools, hospitals, shopping centers, pools, churches, sports fields, fire houses, police stations, theaters, etc. Getting lost was easy for Levittown pioneers to do in sections that resembled each other. Relatives, who came to visit occasionally from Philadelphia and upstate, needed a car escort to show them how to get out of town at the end of the day. Even delivery men would ask us kids for directions on how to get out of the cookie cutter town.

WIWAK there was a big metal mail box on every other street in Levittown for mailing letters. There were also 10-cent pay telephones outside most stores. We didn't have a phone when we moved to Levittown and our family shared a party line with other neighbors.

WIWAK Levittown was built on farm fields in Bucks County, Pa. At night kids could actually go outside and see millions of stars every night because there were not a lot of outside lights flooding the skies. The remaining farms soon disappeared, development of businesses exploded and the skies aren't as clear as they used to be.

WIWAK there was dirt and mud everywhere in the sections and we heard stories about people who actually

81

couldn't find their own houses, because they all looked alike.

WIWAK herds of whitetail deer running through our back lawn was a daily occurrence the first year we moved into our Levittown home.

WIWAK quite a few friends of mine in Levittown whose fathers fought in the Pacific Theater in World War II refused to eat rice. My friends said their fathers would not eat rice because they associated it with the Japanese. None of the Levittown men I knew, who fought in Europe, boycotted pizza or frankfurters.

WIWAK we didn't really have an opinion about people of color in Levittown because they were not part of the community we lived in. When a family tried to integrate into one of the sections, it set off fireworks for a lot of people who really didn't know what they were all about. Some drove by the house to see what they could see and many ignored it. Kids in my neighborhood were oblivious to the discrimination that was taking place in our midst. It wasn't until many years later that the small minority of people who opposed allowing everyone to achieve the American Dream of home ownership were confronted with their own bigotry.

WIWAK many malcontents couldn't wait to get out of our "one-horse town." We did see deer, but none of us ever saw a horse anywhere ever.

WIWAK every house in Levittown was forever identified with the people who lived there first. One of my best friends, Jimmy Karcher, moved several times during his life, but the house he lived at on 8 Nature Lane has always been identified with the Karcher family. It doesn't matter who has lived there since, the house will always have the Karcher moniker.

WIWAK it was difficult to find an unoccupied baseball field on the weekend in Levittown. Before pro-football became the nation's number one sport, baseball was the top game kids liked to play. Organized baseball at the amateur level was very popular. The leagues at all age levels were flooded and they took up all available spaces to practice on the public school fields

Mike Tasker playing stick ball with his brother, Charles-1960's

where we played. If no fields were available for us kids, we played stick ball on the street. But we still benefited from the leagues - bats that cracked during baseball league games were prime bats for playing wall ball. This game involved one kid throwing a heavy rubber ball to a batter standing at a wall. The strike zone was determined by a chalked square drawn on the wall behind the batter. Boundaries determined singles, doubles, triples, home runs, and out of bounds.

WIWAK most Levittowners dressed to the nines for packed Saturday and Sunday services. Sneaks, jeans, and tee shirts were the dress mode of playgrounds. Jackets, shirts, and shorts proclaiming softball champions, vacation retreats, rock n'roll artists, and Madison Avenue products never adorned the faithful.

WIWAK our favorite playground in Levittown was at

Walt Disney Elementary in the Pinewood section. Disney visited the school in 1954 to lay the cornerstone and help dedicate it. This school was the first school ever in the nation to be named for Disney. But that's not what made it so great: it was the authentic World War II United States Navy jet fighter. Many Boomers took turns in that cockpit and played flying that jet in make-believe sorties. Sadly, there were no workable guns for the budding G.I. Joes in the sections, but that did not stop the make-believe heroics. Some of the kids that I helped save the world with in imaginary dogfights later lost their lives in the jungles of Vietnam.

WIWAK every winter we looked forward to a tasty neighborhood delicacy, sucking on the six-foot icicles that hung off our Levittown roofs. The houses did not originally have gutters built onto them, so icicles formed everywhere. Nobody cared if the water that composed most of the icicles came off of roofs that were covered with asbestos shingles, not to mention whatever birds left behind. Many a black and white photo from the 50's and 60's shows kids of all ages smiling and sucking on giant icicles. Could it be the reason why some adults today complain that they've lost their sense of taste?

WIWAK you didn't need a special pass or a trip through a metal detector to see a politician running for president. The first two candidates I saw were John F. Kennedy and Richard M. Nixon at the Levittown Shopping Center. No politician worth his salt at the time would pass up all the Democrats and Republicans living in this new community. The thousands that showed up at the mass rallies got as close as they wanted. I think every Catholic and Irishman showed up at the Kennedy rally the day he spoke in front of Pomeroy's Department Store. Today, the only thing I remember was Kennedy's smile and tan.

Candidate John F. Kennedy campaigned at the Levittown Shopping Center on October 30, 1960

It was the last time we saw any candidate riding in an open limousine.

WIWAK streetlights across Levittown told thousands of Boomers it was time to end play time each night. Some kids, who failed to observe the light reminder, had fathers with distinctive whistles that herded them home each evening.

WIWAK every summer in Levittown would signal the beginning of the great fruit heist. Many families owned their own fruit trees, but fences were not allowed to be more than four feet high. So kids, under cover of darkness, would begin the clandestine fruit harvest: peaches, nectarines, cherries, apples and pears were among the pilfered goodies. The heists (thefts) provided not only the forbidden fruit, but also ammo for bombing roofs of snooty neighbors. But some home-owners fought back. One neighbor actually kept his full-grown Easter duck in his backyard, to keep kids out. That duck sounded the alarm on quite a few juvenile delinquents. But while many kids wouldn't think twice about stealing fruit, not many would lift vegetables from their own family plot.

WIWAK there was only one movie theater, called the Towne Theater, and it was always crowded with hundreds of kids during matinees. At night, young teens and adults packed the air conditioned movie house dressed up in jackets and ties and dresses. When a blockbuster movie was in town, the line wrapped around the entire building. Early in Elvis' career, the line wrapped twice around the entire theater building.

WIWAK there weren't a lot of funerals in the early days of Levittown, since most of the parents were young veterans of World War II. Old people and their maladies were the exception in this culture of youth. Pediatricians were the main doctors in Lower Bucks Hospital, and one doctor actually delivered over 30,000 babies in his career.

WIWAK a new car in the driveway always drew a crowd. Not only was it a chance to see the latest models up close, but to applaud those that could afford a new set of wheels. Seeing one's favorite car in someone else's driveway sure beat dreaming about it in a car magazine.

WIWAK the architects that designed Levittown somehow saw fit to combine the washing machine, oil heater and toilet in the same tiny room.

WIWAK typical families numbered around five per household. Yet, most families only had one toilet to handle the load each and every day. Nobody at this time ever spoke about the urgency for a second toilet. Yet trying to get quality time in the bathroom was at times a battle. Once someone flushed the toilet and opened the door, a battle for entry was on by the next two kids who had been patiently doing the green apple two-step in the living room. Cries of "I was here first" echoed throughout the house. It took bathroom refs called Mom and Dad to settle the messy dispute and determine who had to go the most. Even if nature took care of itself in a quick fashion, making the culprit you just battled wait a considerable amount of time was standard operating procedure. Making the loser whimper and plead for you to hurry up was worth it every time. Before exiting and letting them in, hiding the toilet paper would always end in a pleading voice calling Mom from the bathroom.

WIWAK everybody's dad in Levittown was a member of one social organization or another. The VFW (Veterans of Foreign Wars) and volunteer fire companies were the most visible organizations in town legally allowed to serve beer on Sundays. Most men joined these organizations because they wanted somewhere to wet their whistles on Sundays. In Pennsylvania the Blue Laws prohibited drinking by all other establishments. The law was originally enacted to help keep Sunday a day for attending churches. When the law was eventually changed, membership in social organizations took a precipitous drop and the bars and restaurants picked up customers.

WIWAK Blue Laws in the state also kept most stores closed from Saturday at 5 p.m. until Monday morning. Here, too, Quakers and other religious denominations viewed shopping for clothes not in keeping with the Sabbath. So on Sundays, streets were loaded with kids and dads hanging around the home. For lack of anything better to do, most families took the proverbial "Sunday Drive" to relatives,

87

picnics, and sightseeing.

WIWAK sharpening any athletic skills was usually attained by playing other local athletes in pick-up games at the Levittown pools that had basketball courts. Playing sports all day and night under the lights was a common practice. Kids in their teens would also play adults at the pools and beat them to retain "game" in basketball and baseball. The only way to get knocked off the court was to lose. Playing adults also made kids better players overall. Winning was the only rule in these games. Kids would take time outs during games by smoking with their buddies. The kids who eventually came out of those venues became some of the top athletes in the United States. No coaches, adults, or school programs could match the athletic education learned on those fabled courts and fields. Coaches, who eventually got these prospects, refined their talents and captured world titles by the bushel full. Levittown made quite a name for itself in sports. World Series titles in Little League baseball were won by Levittown American (1960) and nearby Morrisville (1954) Little League teams less than seven years apart. Babe Ruth World Series titles were captured by multiple Levittown teams. Some area kids that played pick-up games of football without pads also went on to play college and pro football.

WIWAK the most wonderful men and women I ever knew were the volunteers that coached, taught, and guided us daily growing up in Levittown. Most of them were decent, hard-working, unpretentious individuals from the "Greatest Generation." They weren't looking out for No. 1, but went out of their way to help every kid in the community.

WIWAK - When I Was A Kid

WIWAK leaving the doors open was commonplace in Levittown. In fact, nobody in my family ever had a key to the house, except my mother. There were times when the door would get locked inadvertently, but that's when we would utilize our climbing skills, entering through a window that was left opened somewhere in the house.

WIWAK sleeping in a tent in the backyard of a Levittown house generally involved draping bedspreads over lawn furniture of one kind or another. A few kids had real tents, but creating plush sleeping quarters for the night kept the rest of us busy. After spending one night in a make-shift tent with little or no sleep, however, we welcomed the following night spent back in our own rooms.

Mike Tasker in his coonskin cap with brother, Charles. Camping in backyard was very popular in early Levittown.

WIWAK the flag of the United States was on permanent display in front of Levittown houses all year long. You could say G.I. Joe lived on every street in early Levittown.

WIWAK nobody I knew had an air conditioner in his house. Some didn't even have fans. If a kid wanted some air, parents told him/her to go outside. As parents made inroads at their jobs, some began to have window units installed. Later on central air conditioning units appeared and some kids were never seen outside again on a hot day. On some hot nights we'd sometimes sleep out on my friend's roof.

WIWAK Levittown was a menagerie of every animal imaginable. Families were constantly acquiring new cats and dogs from neighbors that didn't know what to do with surplus puppies and kittens. Other pet animals included pythons, clown monkeys, rats, mice, groundhogs, hamsters, raccoons, skunks (unscented), chickens, ducks, rabbits, parakeets, hawks, pheasants, quail, lizards, box turtles, fish, piranhas, cockatoos, and tarantulas. Levitt's pioneers would have given Noah a run for his money in those fabulous fifties. It was amazing the variety of pets kids had in those days.

WIWAK we bought rubber rafts and used them to float around Levittown Lake in late spring. The lake was originally dug out by Levitt to help make concrete for his mammoth housing project. On opening day over a thousand people from all over the county would come to try their luck for rainbow, brown and brook trout. But after thousands of anglers had given up on pursuing trout in the former quarry by mid May, we would swim and float out to the middle of the lake. In certain parts of the lake we could stand on a sandbar where the trucks used to drive out to pick up sand and stone. Today the Lakeside Section surrounds this huge lake.

WIWAK building fences and hanging wash out on weekends was prohibited in every section of Levittown. Rumor has it that millionaire Bill Levitt actually drove around his huge development to make sure rules were being adhered to by residents. In the beginning most residents adhered to the sales agreement, but it was eventually ignored by women that had scads of clothes to wash all week for their large families.

WIWAK the smallest window in a Levittown house should have been the largest – the bathroom window. Some of Levittown's model houses had an oil heater inserted right in the bathroom. During hot summer spells the bathroom was not a place to spend a lot of time.

WIWAK the lawns were spacious for most kids that hailed from the city. Levitt put plenty of open spaces in most sections for kids to play. However, most kids were lazy and didn't always want to walk the seven blocks to the fields. Our lawn in front of our house was filled with kids most days playing every game imaginable. Some neighbors did not want kids on their lawn, even their own children. It didn't take long for some neighbors to get into fights over balls that landed on their manicured lawns. Sometimes a so-called "adult" would actually take a ball that landed on his lawn and refuse to give it back until the offender's parent came to get it. It didn't take long before the kids of these "adults" were ostracized by the other neighborhood kids, which led to another confrontation between parents.

Chapter 8

Loving You

"Love is life. And if you miss love, you miss life."

Leo Buscaglia

WIWAK letting the opposite sex know you liked her was a major step toward becoming a full-fledged teenager. Many kids would initiate the first smack at an opportune time, but others utilized an array of unorthodox methods to show their affection: splashing or spitting water in her face, rubbing her face in the snow, punching her in the arm, and grabbing her book bag were favorite methods with the boys, but not terribly popular with the girls. Sometimes writing her name and yours on the street in chalk, or in the snow, or even on your hand in ink got the message across. Shy boys could leave a note on her desk with three names and instructing her to circle the one boy she likes, call her house and not answer when she picks up, walk by her house (today considered stalking), tell her best friend his feelings, or ask his sister to have her sleep over. Bolder boys would carry her books to class, play spin the bottle with her only, or play post office with her only – but by that time, it was serious!

WIWAK nobody we hung out with ever got the opportunity to sleep over their girlfriend's house, even if he told her parents that he loved their daughter more than they did. Simply proposing such an idea to a girlfriend's parents would have resulted in permanent exclusion from ever seeing her again. Parents had one dictum concerning their daughters – If and when you marry her at the proper time, then you can share sleeping quarters with her – no ifs, ands, or butts! There were a few instances, very few in our neighborhood, where a few kids "had" to get married because of a weak moment. Moreover, many of the girls who were going to get married all seemed to become domestic, because we overheard our parents repeatedly talking about them baking buns in the oven.

WIWAK one method of remembering a torrid teen love affair with a girl was to visit a photo booth in a store. As a young kid we'd make silly faces, pose with cigarettes, or make rude hand gestures. With a girl it was a photographic love session. There were four sizzling black and white pictures for only 25-cents. I wonder what happened to those pictures.

WIWAK the most popular girl with the juvenile delinquents in our neighborhood did not resemble Sandra Dee. As young boys we didn't know at first why she was so popular. She smoked, wore heavy makeup, tight jeans, and tight sweaters and had a loose mouth. She definitely made quite a few parents uptight too. We all loved that girl.

WIWAK dances didn't have police security, and everybody dressed normally. Seeing your girlfriend out of a school uniform, hair all done up and in a dress was a special sight to behold! Cursing was practiced among a few base teenagers, but most couples were interested in dancing and having clean fun. Not hearing the "F-bomb" an entire evening and treating my date like a young lady is a treasured memory to this day.

WIWAK my girlfriend smoked cigarettes. We thought it was really neat to have her take a drag of the cigarette, and then I would kiss her and blow out her smoke. I didn't care if my mouth tasted like an astray. I did anything for a kiss – I was a desperate young boy. Smoking wasn't the great taboo then that it is today. Practically everyone smoked.

WIWAK my biggest crush was for Sally Starr, a Philadelphia TV personality. Sally dressed up like a cowgirl with six shooters and daily introduced cartoons of Popeye and the Three Stooges on WFIL Channel Six. She was bigger than Elvis with little kids in Levittown. Once she came to our church fair, arriving in a black Cadillac. Calling all of her "buckaroos" up on stage, she asked us to sing "I'm Popeye, The

Sailor Man" with her. As I began singing I fell off the stage and broke my arm. She helped get me assistance, and to this day I love Sally. I still also love spinach, and, of course, the Stooges.

The GANG'S ALL HERE   Tasker family friend, Mike Pirolli (right) poses with his entire family with popular TV personality, Sally Starr.*

WIWAK parents actually dropped off and picked up their daughters from dances. Did their dads know what we wanted to do with their daughters after the dance? Hey, they were young boys once. Most of us, myself included, had steamy visions of necking for hours with Barbara Ann in some romantic interlude that would make Doris Day and Rock Hudson green with envy. But my girlfriend never had to go "visit her aunt" for a couple of months. Though the dads in those days figured they knew what we were looking for, most of us boys were satisfied with kissing. My girlfriend's father had nothing to worry about. She was one of those "good girls".

WIWAK I fell in love with a new girl each week. My only problem was that I was too shy to inform any of them. My brother and I used to practice how our first kiss with a real girl would go. How'd we do it? We would practice by kissing our hands and acting out the scene for the amusement of each other. When that day came for me in eighth grade, I

*Photo courtesy of Victoria Pirolli.

never thought twice about what to do, and the rest they say is history.

WIWAK a 60's snow storm enabled me to write on the side of a hill my love for a grammar school classmate named Beverly. I did the fancy writing by walking out the letters in the snow. My only problem was I started too late, and it snowed that evening. Later, I got up the nerve to call her house, but when she answered I remained silent. I never got up the courage to tell her in person.

Chapter 9

Boob Tube

**The Rifleman Lucas McCain and Mark McCain
from The Rifleman Series TV show.**

*"If it weren't for Philo T. Farnsworth, inventor
of television, we'd still be eating frozen radio
dinners."*

Johnny Carson

WIWAK national television corporations would never interrupt any regularly scheduled program with a bulletin noting a truck accident somewhere on I-95, a cooking show host getting out of jail, or a thunderstorm in the summertime. When TV stations did interrupt programming, you knew something newsworthy was following, such as the Kennedy assassination, death of some other prominent world figure, or some catastrophic world event.

WIWAK entertainers on television were macho, smoked, drank, and lived with the opposite sex. Though divorce was common in their real lives, their agents usually kept this and all other immoral behavior out of the magazines that chronicled their daily doings. Their addictions eventually ensured eternity so that the next crop of stars could replicate their successes and failures in life.

WIWAK television was black and white and there were only three channels to watch. In order to go from one channel to the other, viewers (kids) had to physically get up off the couch or floor to change the station. Some kids could change from one channel to another at lightning speed, quickly ruining the television knob. Once damaged, the knob needed some creative engineering to keep the channel on. This is where the fun began for many families. One method to ensure channel stability was to put a matchbook cover beneath the knob once a program was selected by everyone. A change of channel required a matchbook readjustment. Besides this problem, sometimes the antenna on the roof needed attention. Yelling out the window in all kinds of weather to the poor boob on the roof trying to fix the reception in the living room was a verifiable comedy routine. If none of these steps helped improve channel reception, nothing worked better than whacking the idiot box on its side to get the picture back on. TVs took so many hits to the side they were soon cracked and dented. Finally, when all else failed, then and only then would 'ma' make a call to the TV repairman – yes, they even made house calls in those days. A house without television was an open invitation to increased sibling rivalries. When the TV repairman with his black case of tubes and wires finally fixed our sick idiot box, we regarded him as a technological genius and wished he could live with us full time.

WIWAK us children controlled the television in my house, not our mother. We heard how other friends were forced to watch what mom and dad wanted and were glad Mom allowed us to pick out the programs.

WIWAK news on television took 15 minutes each evening with one newsman giving all the information. The newsman gave the news without the aid of a cup of coffee or bottle of water. His total concentration was on speaking to the camera and not breaking in any comedy routine with moronic jokes. Viewers didn't know if he was married, had illegitimate kids, was pregnant, or just got back from a vacation. Some news-people actually hold conversations with each other today and forget about viewers at times. After midnight, TV went off the air with a cleric delivering an inspiring message followed by a patriotic scene with the "Star Spangled Banner" playing in the background.

WIWAK by the mid 60's networks started to show films that were only a few years old. This was a treat because up until then the TV public was forced to watch really old movies.

WIWAK shows by the dozen were geared for teenagers.

One of the most prominent shows watched daily by almost every teenager in America was American Bandstand. This show was groundbreaking in that it featured the hottest rock & roll artists, and featured Philadelphia teenagers doing all the latest dances. After the show's disc jockey got caught up in the payola scandals in the mid 1950's, when record producers actually paid off producers to air their records, Dick Clark took the show over and steered it to dazzling show biz heights. Any current movie directors who want to show how teenagers really were in the sixties only have to look at Bandstand to get a true handle on the times. What viewers won't see are malcontents in leathers, or girls half dressed.

WIWAK the one thing that could make people of all ages cease what they were doing in the early 1960's was watching on television a space shot by NASA at Cape Canaveral. The first several astronauts were as big as Elvis and the Beatles.

WIWAK some people would buy anything that was advertised on television regardless of the quality and cost. A product wouldn't go by without one neighbor I knew buying it, if it appeared on TV, he bought it.

WIWAK watching a football game on Monday night on ABC was a gift from the sports gods. It was an event most kids would never forget. ABC was also the same network that brought us sports from around the globe. It was truly amazing for the sports fanatic.

WIWAK one of the biggest heroes of the late 50's had to be George Reeves, whose portrayal of Superman was a hit with millions of kids. Many kids couldn't believe it when he was found dead with a bullet lodged in his head. However, that didn't stop millions of kids from flying around their houses with bathroom towels wrapped around their necks.

WIWAK some of the best comedians of all time plied their trade on television's three networks, and their humor holds up to this day. Legendary comedians included Jackie Gleason, Lou Costello, Milton Berle, Sid Caesar, Jonathan Winters, Jerry Lewis, Steve Allen, Ernie Kovacs, George Burns, Jack Benny, Lucille Ball, and Carol Burnett, to name a few. What was amazing about these greats was that they never depended on base language to get people to laugh. Imagine Lucy throwing "F bombs" at Ricky – I don't think so!

WIWAK my family watched "The Millionaire" on TV religiously. The program consisted of a millionaire picking a name out of the phone book and his courier, Anthony, delivering a check. The show would then follow the people and tell what they did with their windfall. They say you don't miss what you don't have, but a few more dollars would have really helped our situation at home. However, Michael Anthony never stopped by to inform us we were filthy rich.

WIWAK the influence of religion showed up on the boob tube. Every week my family would watch Bishop Fulton J. Sheen on his #1 rated TV show, "Life is Worth Living."

WIWAK it seemed that every comedian on television had to know how to handle a six-shooter, do impressions, and be sponsored by a cigarette company.

WIWAK most television personalities tried to drive home the idea between Let's Make A Deal and Queen for a Day that ice boxes were called refrigerators. You know you're talking to a Boomer when he uses the words "ice box." I could never understand how women would go crazy over being awarded an ice box. A new car, yes! An ice box, I don't think so.

Chapter 10

Communicating

Twenty-two students cramming into a telephone booth trying to establish a stacking record. St. Mary's College-Moraga, California 1959*

"Me, we."
Muhammad Ali

* Photo from Joe Munroe-Ohio Historical Collections

WIWAK my entire family pulled no punches when it came to communicating with one another over the telephone that a loved one had earned his wings. Dead was dead and that's how the news was conveyed. Euphemisms such as buying the farm, kicking the bucket, going to a better place, checking out, and passing away were rare in the family when they made contact with one another. And, everyone went to the Irish wake, which had a festive air about it.

WIWAK most parents wanted to know where we were going. We knew where they were going every day of their boring existence, so we never asked them. Yet, when they asked for a specific destination, we'd always reply, "Out." The truth be known, most of us really didn't have a clue where we were going either. Some wiseacre would say "Out" is close by "Nowhere," south of town next to the "I Don't Know" café. But we never tried that one. One night my mother stopped my older brother immediately after he gave her the one word reply. "Tonight," she proclaimed, "I want to know once and for all exactly where 'out' is." My brother never cracked and we all smirked at one another as he exited the house. Years later, my brother reported to us he tried the same routine with his new wife, but he didn't succeed once. Apparently, "Out" only works on parents.

WIWAK most mothers were smart enough to have the telephone installed near the kitchen where all conversations could be monitored. It was funny for the younger kids in the house watching older brothers and sisters trying to talk on the phone within earshot of mom. It was the only time of the day when teenagers all over America would repeat the same five words to the person on the receiving end of the line – "I can't talk right now."

WIWAK phones were a lifeline for kids with working mothers, especially during the summer. A call to mom during the last two hours of her workday was essential for younger kids to help stop older siblings from killing them. Kids didn't care if mom's concentration on her work was shattered. However, nobody that had a working mom ever considered contacting dad at work to settle such disputes. It was a given that kids who assaulted each other on a daily basis knew placing such a call would certainly result in dad kicking everybody's rear upon his arrival at home sweet home. Phones had the familiar stickers on them with emergency phone numbers – police, fire and poison – but dad's work number had an X marked through it. As far as the "old man" was concerned, you didn't exist when he was out scraping up a buck in the jungle each day.

WIWAK many children were salespeople for local radio stations, and they neither knew nor got paid for their efforts. Every time someone would reach out to touch them by phone, they became ambassadors for local radio. Stations would run promotions that promised a thousand dollar prize if you answered the phone with their call letters, for instance "I listen to WFIL" instead of "Hello." Some stations let the jackpot grow and grow until someone answered correctly. When the prize ran into the thousands, that's all kids would talk about each day. The person who thought up this marketing campaign hit gold, because everyone answered the phone with the familiar refrain whether they listened to the station or not.

WIWAK my mother never had to explain the meaning of "no" to us.

WIWAK contraptions didn't always work right, and we would invariably utilize our communication skills with the offending inanimate object. Whatever didn't work we surmised could be made to work by hitting it and yelling, "C'mon!" If the problem didn't work right away, "C'mon!" was usually followed by yelling louder, "You don't want to work? Well, you're going to work!" It was common to see people with red exasperated faces hitting and yelling at soda dispensers, TVs, car engines, and juke boxes.

WIWAK I continually asked my mother the exact location of Heaven, and what she thought it would be like. I don't know why, but most mothers feel they can answer a question from their kid that philosophers have pondered over for centuries. My mother, who did a fairly good job raising five offspring, said it was a place where we'd be reunited forever, if we're good, with dad, family, friends, and Jesus. My family got along well, and I missed friends and family that were no longer around. So, I liked her explanation and looked forward to that eventuality. Yet, I worried about some of the families I knew that didn't hit it off too well with each other during holidays and special occasions. Every block had one of those families that must have missed school on the day they were teaching Communications 101. Face it, hanging out with family for eternity is not as easy as putting up with each other for a few hours on Thanksgiving Day and Christmas on earth. I was certain such families would be paid multiple visits by Heaven's Angel Peace Department officers once the wine started to flow. To this day I still wonder if blood stains clouds in Heaven.

WIWAK most kids had colorful imaginations each time they swore in public. Using four letter words was the exception in those days when trying to communicate with a friend. Usually such language was only used by base characters. Some barbs included the following: "You're full of soup!" "Drop dead!" "Jesus H. Jackson!" Son of a gun!" "Cheese 'N Rice!" "Jimminy Crickets!" "Oh fudge!" "God darn it!" "Jumpin' johosefat!" "Dog gonnit!" Dag nabbit!" etc...

WIWAK nobody I knew ever cursed in front of his/her mom and dad when speaking with a friend – never, never, never, ever!!! You knew who was around you and where you were. Most kids in those days could express themselves without cursing.

WIWAK my friend, Ray, had a difficult time communicating with us, and in school he had problems passing tests. The teachers couldn't seem to figure out Ray's problem, but we didn't care if Ray knew anything, since he made us laugh all year long. Ray had a way with the English language and fractured it on a regular basis to our glee. At Christmas time we would just sit back and listen to Ray's versions of holiday classics. You haven't lived until you heard Ray belting out "O Come Augie Faithful." Ray crooned that we should "Crown thy Virgin" in "Silent Night," and that "bows (not boughs) holly" are found in the lyrics of "Tis the season to be jolly." Proud of his Italian heritage, Ray loved Dean Martin singing "Winter Wonderland." Ray's version, however, was titled "Window Wonderland." Everyday during morning prayers at Catholic school, Ray would start his Hail Mary with the words, "Hello, Mary!" The top-10 music list wasn't spared by Ray, since he informed us that "Louie, Louie" was "gay" (happy) and "Poetry in Motion" was in fact called, "Oh, A Tree in Motion." Ray also had his own version of the "Name Game" by Shirley Ellis, but that's another story.

WIWAK we could pick out where our friends were originally from the moment they spoke. Upstate Pennsylvania expressions and Philly expressions are easy to pick out. Since most kids were from one of the two areas, in my neighborhood it was easy to pick out colloquial expressions. Some examples of Philly expressions were: "Akame" (Acme), "Use guys" (You guys), "Gimme a Coke" (Give me a Coke), "Whatsamada wit you" (What's the matter with you), and "I ain't got no" (I don't have any). An up-stater would say, "Turn on the earl burner" (Turn on the oil burner.) One time my family took a trip to the 1964 World's Fair in New York City and the waiter at the restaurant could tell where we were from immediately after we asked for Cokes. He was from Philly and knew we hailed from his hometown.

WIWAK our other mother, Ma Bell, provided us with our one link to the outside world, especially with the kids we left in our old neighborhood. Eventually we lost touch with one another, but the phone was constantly ringing with our new friends. It was always fun to watch siblings racing for a ringing phone screaming, "I got it!"

WIWAK I didn't recognize my sister's annual school portrait. The problem was she didn't have a telephone attached to ear. It always amazed me how girls in general would have anything else to communicate about, after spending all day talking to each other in school. I guess I had a lot to learn about the opposite sex.

WIWAK our family was always communicating about everything. The main subject we loved to talk over was what we were going to eat for the next meal. I guess when there wasn't an overabundant amount of food in the house, it naturally consumes a lot of mental attention. The odd thing about it was that we started talking about the next meal before we were halfway through the meal in front of us! Now, I'm sure the Rockefellers talked money management and filling their portfolios, but we talked about stuffing our mouths. Call it lack of security, but this popular pastime continues to this very day.

WIWAK hardly anyone in the section where we lived divorced. All of my buddies had both parents. Whether they were happily married was up for debate. If a divorced woman moved into the neighborhood, everyone, I mean everyone, seemed to know where she lived. And if a marriage dissolved, communication outlets lit up throughout the section. There was always one neighbor who was the Gladys Kravitz (nosy body from the sit-com "Bewitched") of the street. These ladies made it their business to know the whole shebang about everybody, especially divorced women. They spread the gossip like a farmer spreads manure. Parents constantly admonished children never to tell these busy-bodies anything, or hold open conversations. My mother told us they were always "fishing" for news, which confused me, because they were never wearing waders or carrying a pole.

WIWAK sending hundreds of Christmas cards in the mail was an annual event for most families that wanted to communicate best wishes during the holiday season. It only cost pennies to mail the Yuletide greetings. Lists of people you sent cards to were usually posted on the inside of the card box from the previous year; nobody wanted to forget who sent them greetings the year before. The mailman would bring over a hundred cards to us, and Ma didn't want to slight anyone. Hanging all of the cards throughout the house was part of the indoor holiday decorations. Those people who sent outstanding cards had their cards placed on our house door. Some friends and relatives who came over during the holidays went out of their way to see where their card was placed. Other families weren't content to hang them around the house, and created elaborate Christmas Trees out of greeting cards.

WIWAK we played games on the phone by bothering other people and not getting into trouble for it. Posing as an electric company employee and asking if a person's refrigerator was running, or if they had 'Prince Albert in a can' were standard jokes we forced on unsuspecting people. We really didn't realize what rubes we really were, and we were the fools people spoke about when they suggested some people needed to get a life.

WIWAK - When I Was A Kid

WIWAK telephones helped us communicate daily and came in as many colors as Henry Ford's Model T – black. Our phone was heavy and the chord was always knotted up. My sister would constantly twirl the chord unconsciously while talking on the phone. Trying to walk more than one foot away from the receiver was an impossibility. We were mesmerized by rumors that rich people in the neighborhood had two phones, including a touch phone that lit up in the dark. The only extravagant thing we did with the phone was calling up information to ask for a number, instead of searching the phone book. We thought we were clever using the phone to call up people with famous names and asking stupid questions.

WIWAK communicating with parents and adults by their first names was a no-no. Some kids got away with it with some individuals, but most adults insisted on propriety.

Chapter 11

Family Stories

Fifties kids playing in the snow in Levittown- Mike Tasker, foreground- from left, Charles Tasker- Jean Tasker, Jimmy Pascoe, Bob Tasker

"The other night I ate at a real nice family restaurant. Every table had an argument going."

George Carlin

WIWAK - When I Was A Kid

WIWAK jelly was a mainstay for our family at home in summertime. One drawback to home-made jelly was the wax that mothers used to can the stuff. If you didn't remove the wax carefully, hundreds of bits of paraffin wax would wind up in your mouth each and every time you used the jelly. Most of the fruit used to can jelly was taken from the countless fruit trees developer William Levitt planted in each lawn. My mother and others were constantly canning and sharing recipes each summer with one another. Resembling early survivalists, some mothers canned so much jelly that their grandchildren are probably still trying to polish it off today.

WIWAK my mother thought nothing of allowing my 13-year-old brother to buy a train ticket and go see his old friends back in Philly. Not only was he street smart, he also knew how to make connections on buses and the 'el.' Some older kids that left friends back in the 'old neighborhood' would do anything to see their old buddies.

WIWAK our family's dining and encyclopedia sets were never full and complete sets. Each week stores would offer dishes and books that would help the family eat and study with the most recent offerings from Madison Avenue. However, somewhere along the line my mom would miss a certain dish piece, or only have the books up to "L" in the encyclopedia offerings. So, eating on different color plate designs was ordinary, and nobody asked for information that began with letters M through Z.

WIWAK the most photographed kid in each family always seemed to be the first born child. The second through seventh kids could be handsomer, prettier, wittier, and smarter, but there was always a plethora of pictures of the first baby the stork dropped off to newlyweds. Usually the last child in these very large families had his/her pictures filed away in the junk drawer with the string, paper and rubber bands. Just ask any kid from a large family, if you don't believe me.

WIWAK catching a house-fly in flight in your hand was a talent most kids admired, but one that few had. My brother, Charles, not only caught countless bugs in mid-flight, but also smacked bees without missing.

WIWAK it was really crucial to us to nail down who in the family could eat the hottest pepper. It was kind of easy to figure out who was the best athlete in the three major sports – basketball, football and baseball. All we had to do was count up the trophies. It was quite another thing to determine who the "King of Peppers" was. If competition had to result in someone hurling up his stomach contents during the heat of battle (pun intended), so be it. We didn't care if the contestants lost their sense of taste vying for the crown. Such goings-on added to the eventual champion's status around our section.

WIWAK a flashlight and someone adept at making shadow animals on the wall with his fingers were all that was needed to entertain us on a hot summer night. My brothers were always willing entertainers, and I was always a good audience.

WIWAK certain houses and kids were off limits to us and we were never told why by my mother.

WIWAK - When I Was A Kid

WIWAK sharing a soda was something my one brother, Charles, and I were always doing at home. Splitting the sugar water equally was crucial. Any violation of the rules would send me crying to my mother for justice. If we were out and combined our nickels to buy one soda, we would agree upon a line on the Pepsi bottle, and before taking that first swig, we would always wipe the bottle rim with our shirt to kill any germs that happened to be present. I never trusted my older brother to split things.

WIWAK the most frustrating contraption ever devised by adults for kids during the winter months was galoshes. Like the Model T automobile, they came in only one color – black! Trying to get the rubberized shoe covers with metal fasteners on required the combined strength of Steve Reeves, Johnny Weissmuller and Charles Atlas. Nobody I knew in my family could get them on easily without sweating. After a few hours battling kids outside into the snow, getting the black rubbers off again would drive kids close to their first nervous breakdown. Once inside a warm house with wet clothes and numb fingers, removing frozen galoshes required adult help. Many a kid undoubtedly let his first curse slip out as Mom or Dad struggled to pull the black monsters off their feet. Breaking the ice and snow on the metal clips was crucial to a successful extraction and becoming galosh-free once again.

WIWAK playing road bingo helped time pass by on long trips by car with my family. Road bingo is played on pre-printed bingo cards listing things you might see on American roadways. Another popular pastime was getting truckers to honk their horns. One game that made it legal to hit your brother and sister in the arm was when we saw a passing car with only one headlight working. Another game was recording how many plates from different states you could see. However, no matter how many games we played in the car, there was always a fight of one kind or another. I wish I had a dime for every time my mother threatened us with, "If I have to stop this car!"

WIWAK each family we knew had a bare minimum of three kids.

WIWAK Mom would occasionally go out and leave my older brother in charge for the evening. As soon as she closed the door to leave, you would have thought a bell went off. It's amazing to watch how kids behave when the main authority figure isn't lurking around the house. In one night my sister suffered a dart in her leg, my brother broke a guitar, the family pet, Inky, suffered a broken paw, and I lost a close one-round boxing bout with towel gloves to my brother. Mom didn't go out again for some time after this one terrible night.

WIWAK we didn't know it, but our mom was setting us all up for high blood pressure, heart disease, diabetes, and strokes. Mom was a food pusher and fed us the same food she grew up on, even though most of our uncles and aunts died in their early fifties. Never making the connections with diet and longevity, Mom only had two seasonings in her recipes that she used quite liberally with every meal – salt and pepper. If something didn't have taste to it, salt was the primary remedy. Who combined fried bologna with melted cheese? Mom. Who brought us that heart sludge condiment

Karo Syrup? Mom. Who taught us that sprinkling salt on everything from cantaloupe to watermelon was normal? Mom. Who advised us to toast and butter pound cake with salted butter? Mom. White bread with sugar covering its surface? Mom. It's no wonder why so many members of Mom's family earned their wings at an early age.

WIWAK shiny bicycles were the most treasured possession in my family. We would plead and cry aloud each Christmas season for a new set of wheels. We wouldn't care if visitors stared at us as we begged Mom and said, "I'll never want another thing in my life if you buy me that bike." As a kid you knew that was a bold face lie, and couldn't believe that Mom really bought that dumb line each year. When the bike showed up in the living room beneath the Christmas tree, it reaffirmed for each con artist that there was indeed a God in heaven. Months later that bike that I wiped down and brought into the house initially each night was unrecognizable in the rusty and dented hunk of junk lying on the front lawn in all types of weather. That same, perfect new bike was now missing a kick stand, fenders, reflectors, and one pedal. Well, Christmas was only four months away. It was time to brush off the old routine and start nagging dear old Mom.

WIWAK the worst torture I could experience other than a visit to the neighborhood dentist was a pink belly. My brothers would hold me down and slap my belly until I couldn't take any more. Worse than Indian burns and Chinese water torture techniques, yes, we tried both on one another, pink bellies were a weekly gift older brothers never forgot to give to the weaker members in my family.

WIWAK everybody in my family past the age of 16 years old smoked. It was a plain simple fact and rite of passage in America at that time. The hardest part of smoking for my brothers came the first time they lit up after dinner in front of Mom. Their faces were as red as the beets we had just eaten, yet we looked up to our older brothers as grown-ups now that they smoked. Since the younger kids in the family still couldn't smoke, nothing was more "boss" than buying candy cigarettes and acting like grownups. Putting candy cigarette packs in our shirts and mimicking our uncles was cool. What could get loads of laughs was acting like you were hacking, spitting huge clumps into white tissue, and struggling for your next breath of air between drags. For some odd reason the people who suffered all the common smoking maladies got a huge laugh out of our performances. Dear 'old' uncle Jim, a prolific chain smoker, only needed one match per day during his brief life to get started each morning on his cigarette habit. Jim was never photographed without a "Murph" hanging from his nicotine stained lips. Coffin nails also made great props when aspiring to imitate Bogie (Humphrey Bogart) in Casablanca. The only similarity between Bogie and most of my aunts and uncles was that they died relatively young from smoking related diseases. Furthermore, it was common to attend funerals of loved ones and see relatives slipping a carton of their favorite cigarettes into their coffin for the journey to the hereafter. What really struck me as funny when I was a kid was seeing Uncle Jim without a smoke dangling from his cold, dead lips. Let's face it, if they insisted on putting glasses on his dead body, then it made sense to really make Jim look like he did in real life by sticking a Murph in his mouth!

WIWAK mud pies were the dessert of choice for my sister, Jean, on a summer afternoon. Some days my sister and her friend would spice up the chocolate treat with garnish –Willow Tree leaves and bugs. At night, pies were lit up with lightning bugs to simulate a birthday party for imaginary guests. Both young girls would also sing Doris Day's hit "Que Sera, Que Sera," during their muddy chores.

WIWAK in my family earmuffs were a common and practical piece of clothing worn by boys and girls on cold winter days. My brothers were always looking for new ways to torture me and liked to use their fingers to snap the "hangy-down" part on my cold ears when I forgot to wear ear muffs. Sometimes I would forgo muffs and wear a hat that had huge bunny flaps to keep my head warm.

WIWAK my mother put one meal on the dinner table and everybody ate it. Skipping dinner usually meant not eating anything until the next morning. There's something to be said for sitting down as a family with only one entrée. "Freedom of Choice" was years off in the future, and most mothers were very good cooks. The featured drink most nights was milk, or water from the tap.

WIWAK S&H Green Stamps probably had a picture of my mother on the wall, she was there so much. S&H was all the rage among people saving up for household items. Of course, my mother usually wanted something for the home, while I always wanted a toy of some kind. Gluing the stamps into the booklets was a lot of fun and I thought I was a big help to my mother. Completing a book helped drive home the concept that everything comes in time. Licking the stamps left an awful taste in my mouth, but I wanted to get a special product. What did I want? Going into first grade I wanted a new metal lunch pail of an elephant holding balloons. Well, Ma saved enough stamps to get the pail and I couldn't wait for opening day of school. Lunch finally came on that initial day of school and I proudly pulled out my pail, but it was not like the ones a majority of kids had in class. Theirs had action figures and TV stars on them, and mine suddenly lost its luster. It wasn't long before some boy noticed my pachyderm-embossed pail and pointed it out to everyone. I could have trekked to an elephant burial ground and died! The next day I took my thermos bottle, which cracked soon after, in a brown paper bag and put the elephant box in permanent storage. Some things you never forget.

WIWAK pets were a valued part of the family, but they were still viewed as animals. My family usually got dogs from people who were giving away pups. There were no arbiters that decided a family's suitability for ownership. Mom usually took care of the pooch as soon as everyone else in the family lost interest when the dog wasn't a cute puppy any longer. We had our share of animals over the years. One stands out among the menagerie, though: Ginger. One morning we woke up and I thought it had snowed during the night in our living room. It turned out that Ginger had chewed the stuffing out of all my mother's living room furniture. When we came home from school, mom said old Ginger had run away. Years later, Mom confessed that Ginger was taken to the pound on a rope. When the pound officials asked if it was her dog, she replied that the dog was hanging around the house and that it might be somebody's from the neighborhood.

WIWAK Spam was a weekly meal that some in my family loved covered with melted cheese. It was not long before I learned from guys in the neighborhood that Spam smelled like dog food, and anyone that ate it had canine tendencies. Dying to fit in, I concurred that it wasn't even fit for dogs. The truth of the matter was that my family would eat almost anything put on the table. The only meal we all boycotted was liver and onions. No measure of gravy could disguise Mom's attempts to get us to eat it.

WIWAK home was a place where silence was a scarce commodity. Mom said she missed the noise when we finally all were at school. She believes the daily goings-on and racket we generated kept her young. Mom also pointed out that living in a big family would help us deal with those people we would meet in the work-world.

WIWAK getting dressed up for Halloween was a family activity. Most outfits came from the house and not off the shelf of some five-and-dime store. Preparation for Halloween usually didn't begin until the day it arrived. Sitting around and trying to figure out what we wanted to be usually involved a trip to the closet and a piece of burnt cork. It was simple and a lot of fun.

WIWAK I could hardly afford anything that would knock my mom's socks off at Christmas, but my siblings and I would pull together and buy Ma some inexpensive perfume, toiletries, slippers, or a housecoat. My mother would go on and on about how much she loved the gift. Subconsciously we were telling Mom to relax, take a bath, put on her slippers, and take it easy from caring for us. Years later she said the perfume (Midnight in Paris) almost made her gag, and that she never liked wearing slippers and housecoats. Yet she played the game perfectly, as most mothers do with their offspring.

WIWAK a game of Jax would keep my family busy for days when we got them. Some kids couldn't get past "threesies", but we tried to perfect our game each day. The only down-side to Jax was when someone in the family found one by stepping on it with no shoes on. They also weren't good if a family had infants crawling around on the floor.

WIWAK slurping down a bottle of Coke was the perfect aid to helping someone in our family let loose an atomic burp, or speak in "Burpease." Of course, who could forget the old adage, "Why toot and waste it, when you can burp and taste it!"

WIWAK trips to Atlantic City in New Jersey were a yearly affair. One thing my brother and I couldn't get enough of was standing in front of the motor cars that would transport people back and forth on the seven mile boardwalk. Doing this would force the driver to push a button that would announce, "Watch the tram car, please!" I'm positive the operators would have run over quite a few brats daily on the boardwalk, if they could have gotten away with it. We never failed to visit Steele Pier and watch the diving horse. There was usually a woman on the horse and it would actually jump off a platform into the ocean below. Later, we would take a trip to the bottom of the ocean on a diving bell. I always ended my visit with some salt water taffy and a frozen chocolate banana.

WIWAK building a snowman together always made for a fun family time.

WIWAK driving Mom crazy was simple by standing in between a screened door and the house. Each day Mom would chime a million times, "Either in or out!" In

Winter Fun! –from left –Mike Tasker, Jimmy Pascoe, Mrs. Tasker and Jean Tasker

the summer the warning changed to, "Shut the door! You're letting the flies in!"

WIWAK whatever Levittown offered my family in the way of recreation was used to the hilt. It didn't take much to make us happy, since we were happy with what we had. Just spending time together as a family was something we all treasured. When the pools got lights for night swimming, we asked ourselves, "What will they think of next?"

WIWAK building a snow fort was a family exercise. The snow had barely stopped falling and we were all out in front of the house building the fort one snow brick at a time. It didn't take long, however, before we got tired of just sitting in our homemade igloos. Soon the boys were choosing up sides for the snowball fight of all snowball fights. During the heat of battle, hands became frozen, and changes of

123

gloves permitted extended snowball throwing in order to conquer the enemy. Unfortunately, some forts didn't make it through the night, because some bratty kids would come by and stomp them.

WIWAK sunburn was part of growing up in the fifties and sixties. Most Irish Americans are prone to sunburn, but keeping an eye on oneself and siblings helped stop severe burning from taking place. For us, however, playing outside was always better than sitting in the house. Kids recovering from sunburns found themselves being peeled by kids who liked to remove dead skin. Irish kids learned early that foggy climates and nice cool days in the fall are their natural habitat.

WIWAK we'd sit around sometimes on the edge of boredom. To make the time pass we would tell each other what we would do for a million dollars, which was a lot of dead presidents back then. Some things we thought up for a million dollars bordered on the ridiculous but it was one that challenged our youthful imaginations and us into hysterics. Another game we came up with to make each other laugh was a game called Make Me Laugh. We'd sit for a long time just trying to make each other laugh with funny faces and weird noises. We were always thinking of ways to amuse ourselves and others.

WIWAK imitating movie, stage, and television stars accorded good mimics instant neighborhood celebrity status. Many kids could duplicate an array of stars, but my brother, Charles, was the only kid around who could nail Johnny Weissmuller's Tarzan call. His yelping always brought the house down, that is, until puberty robbed him of this unique talent. Later he perfected Ed Sullivan and Topo Gigio, but many still remember him for his Tarzan to this very day. That's entertainment!

WIWAK colognes Jean Nate and Hai Karate were two things the teens in my family couldn't do without. Some drenched themselves in their cologne and you could smell them a minute before you actually caught sight of them.

WIWAK a doctor visited my family when one of us got really sick. We knew our doctor on a first name basis, and he didn't think he was a god of some kind. Furthermore, some of us knew his kids and he actually lived in a middle class neighborhood, coached Little League baseball, spoke fluent English and drove an American car.

WIWAK my boyhood home had a certain smell all of its own. To this day you could blindfold me and put me in it and I'd know I was home. Some other houses of friends I hung with also elicit good memories, while others conjure up smells of onions, cabbage, garlic, and monkey do-do.

WIWAK nobody made tears go away quicker than my Mom did. Most mothers had this quality; any injury or slight would find Mom's arms open wide as a child entered the door sobbing. Of course, boys who had fathers said their "old man" would say, "Stop crying, or I'll give you something to cry about!" If my mother found out I was beaten up by an older boy, Mom was not above sending out my older brothers to even the score. It was nice sometimes being the baby of the family. Thanks a lot, Mom!

WIWAK taking off our uniforms began as soon as we

entered the door after school. We set records putting on play clothes. Unlike today, there were a lot more things to do outside than inside the typical Baby Boomer's house.

WIWAK my older brothers would grab me and slap me around with my own hands. While they were whacking me, they'd keep saying, "Stop hitting yourself." I thought it would never end, but one day I grew taller and larger than all of my antagonists. I often thought about beating up each and every one of my brothers one day, but there was that older brother syndrome in my mind, and I just couldn't take any of them.

WIWAK the most read magazine in our house was not Life, Time, or Reader's Digest. Like most other Boomers, "Mad" magazine was a hot pick at the drug store.

WIWAK my mother would take tomatoes that hadn't turned red by October and wrap them in newspaper and put them in the upstairs. Eventually they would turn red and we'd enjoy them into Thanksgiving and early December. How people could not see the advantages of home grown vegetables was beyond me. I thought people eating store-bought tomatoes were foolish. Store-bought tomatoes were labeled garbage in my house. But I'm certain the people I ridiculed called us "farmers" behind our backs.

Author Mike Tasker in the family garden picking tomatoes in his madras shorts- early 1960's.

Chapter 12

Culture

1950's children competing in a hula hoop contest.

"It's ironic that in our culture everyone's biggest complaint is about having enough time; yet nothing terrifies us more than the thought of eternity."

Dennis Miller

WIWAK Elvis had "it!" Most kids really couldn't explain what "it" really was, but most agreed they knew "it" when they saw "it." Others that had "it" splashed all over them in ample portions in the world of music were the Beatles and Frank Sinatra.

* Photo - http://www.wikipedia.com

WIWAK the athlete that transcended all sports like no other before or since was Muhammad Ali. This was a fact, not an opinion, held by a majority of people around the world. Never had an athlete caused such a commotion among sports fanatics.

WIWAK acting out what we just saw on the movie screen was a given once we got outside. It was amazing to see hundreds of kids battle each other like Kirk Douglas in our best Spartacus imitation after a matinee that cost 35 cents. It didn't take much imagination for adults to figure that their kids had just caught a Dracula flick when they saw hundreds of kids running to waiting cars while trying to take a nip out of each others' throats.

WIWAK there was nothing more repulsive than someone blowing his nose with a handkerchief and putting it back into his pocket in school. Mothers would try to emulate the perfect mothers portrayed on mindless television shows. Hours of each day would be devoted to ironing everything from drapes, tablecloths, underwear and handkerchiefs. Madison Avenue convinced millions of women that happiness could be obtained with a dust cloth and toilet bowl brush.

WIWAK Hercules with Steve Reeves will always remain the best Hercules for many in the Baby Boom generation. Besides Johnny Weissmuller of Tarzan fame, he was the first male stud girls ever saw in a loin cloth.

WIWAK joining a gang that was bent on causing trouble in your neighborhood was not part of our culture. You didn't have to be a rocket scientist to know that if you did anything in Levittown, most people knew who you were. If they didn't know you, they knew someone who did. Besides, the boss of all bosses always holding court in my house each day didn't go by the name of Vito, Angelo, or Carlo – her name was M-O-M.

WIWAK communists were said to be lurking behind everything that was bad for America. Some said chlorinated water was a "Commie plot!" Most Baby Boomers smile with a full set of beautiful teeth when this fact is recounted.

WIWAK most kids believed in the Easter Bunny, Santa Claus, Tooth Fairy and ghosts. Even when Santa was appearing simultaneously in the Macy's Thanksgiving Day Parade in New York City and Gimbel's turkey extravaganza in Philadelphia, we didn't question why. The whole house of cards eventually came crumbling down for me, when I was allowed to stay up late with everyone else one Christmas Eve. In years' past I was told only adults stayed up late to help welcome Santa when he landed in our neighborhood. Now I was being asked to help wrap up gifts for nephews, and welcome neighbors stopping in the house for a Christmas Eve visit; neighbors who helped themselves to cookies previously reserved for Santa. What happened? Staying up and hanging out with the adults wasn't as much fun as I once thought it was. The adults in my house were also telling me that there was no such rodent called the Easter Bunny, and that Fairies of any kind were to be avoided at all costs – not that there was anything wrong with them. I still believe in ghosts...

WIWAK the moon landing in the late 60's was the biggest thing that ever happened up to that time. Most kids couldn't get enough of the astronauts and the space program. Let's face it, these guys put us onto Tang. We were crazy about them.

WIWAK aunts and uncles seemed to have a preoccupation with the culture of death. Maybe it was a result of all the bloodshed that took place in their lifetimes. Maybe it was a result of the short life spans that their parents had. They'd think nothing of taking us for a ride to the local cemetery before stopping for an ice cream at a local custard stand. Like the Boy Scouts of America, they believed in being "prepared." What seemed gory to us was not so much visiting the dead, but stopping by their own headstone with their names printed on it. The date was unfinished with only the numeral "19". One thing some of them never counted on was living into the 21st century.

WIWAK Christopher Columbus was a hero; we even got a day off from school. God bless the Italians.

WIWAK the plasticization of America had not yet begun. It was routine to eat on real plates and drink our favorite drinks from glass containers. When television personalities enjoyed a cup of something, they did it properly, from a cup sitting on a saucer. Looking back it's hard to imagine Marilyn Monroe, Elizabeth Taylor, Jane Mansfield or Ava Gardner sucking water from a bottle of Poland Spring and gabbing with talk show host Jack Paar.

WIWAK people used to take the time and effort to dress properly before going out to work or play. During the heat of the summer it was not unusual to see men in ties and summer jackets. Men didn't try to emulate kids' fashions.

Women took extreme pride in their appearance, especially on Saturday nights.

WIWAK devouring large amounts of food was considered to be a healthy appetite, and nobody was counting caloric intake. One food that took on mythical proportions in our area was an ice cream concoction from Greenwood Dairies called a "Pig's Dinner." Risking a brain freeze, many kids bugged their families to take them to Greenwood Dairy to take on the ice cream behemoth. Eating the whole thing all alone would result in no charge. The dessert was ice cream scoops on bananas covered in whipped cream and sauce.

WIWAK ladies had their own entrance into area bars and restaurants. In most taprooms women were not allowed or encouraged to sit at the bar. The reason given was that it was not lady-like to walk in alone to a taproom. My mother always took us through the ladies entrance to get some excellent food in the taproom. This arrangement allowed bar owners to enhance their profit line by letting families eat in separate rooms, away from vulgar language out in the tap room.

WIWAK fireworks were illegal in the state of Pennsylvania, but it always seemed like kids had crackers of all kinds all year long. Every Fourth of July people swore some neighbors were trying to recreate the Battle of Gettysburg with their pyrotechnic displays.

WIWAK most entertainment took place outside the home and people flocked by the thousands to see their local athletic stars. The most attended sporting event was high school football. Bucks County spawned nationally ranked powerhouses like Neshaminy and Bishop Egan high schools. Area stadiums were built to accommodate the huge crowds that came out to see them perform. Dozens of professional football players emerged from these grid programs.

WIWAK most people listened to AM on the radio dial. Nobody listened on FM until the mid 1960's. Before the advent of hard rock, FM featured music your parents would listen to. Once kids picked up on FM, AM radio began to lose its influence with teenagers.

WIWAK rock and roll was king. Most music was made for dancing to, and drugs were only given out by doctors to sick people. The 45's and 33 1/3 albums our songs came packaged in had pictures and liner notes about our favorite singers. We'd sit playing our records and looking at those pictures for hours, days, months on end. Some of us took great care of our records, while others

1950's record player and 33⅓ album

mishandled their collections and records became scratched and played like the artists were singing in the rain. Inviting buddies to your house to hang out and listen to records was a teenage pastime. Handling records the right way without putting your fingers on the record ensured a clearer sound. Paraphernalia for keeping records clean included waxes, cleaners, brushes etc. Some kids became known for their extensive record collections, while others became experts in identifying song titles, groups, writers, producers, record labels etc. Finally, rock & roll records enabled kids to practice the latest dance moves at home before testing their talents at parties and neighborhood dances.

WIWAK we didn't have helmets or protection of any kind for riding bikes, wagons, go carts, or sleds. Most of us knew riding was just another risk in our daily lives. Dads who went around the world and fought WWII viewed our games as harmless fun. Helmets? Forget about it!

WIWAK it was fun to meet your buddies from the neighborhood at the area drive-in movies. Once we got together, we'd fly over to the playground beneath the giant outdoor screen. As soon as it started to get dark, the previews would start and we always stuck our fingers in front of the projector. If the first movie was a clunker, we'd run around the craggy asphalt lot spying on older teenagers making their moves on girls. Some cars were packed with teenagers and many kids got into the drive-in by hiding in the back trunk, or under covers on the floor of the car. We usually brought our drinks and snacks to the drive-in and couldn't believe the cost of things at the overpriced concession stand.

WIWAK during the mid sixties everything seemed to be changing in the American landscape. Marriage was no different. All the rules changed as I stood on the precipice of adulthood. My best friend's dad took me, his son, and another friend, Jimmy, for ice cream on the way home from a fishing trip to the shore. We stopped at some dive on a road in the Jersey Pines, and parked in the lot. In an open convertible was Jimmy's dad having a scoop or two with his girlfriend – not his mother. As we pulled out of the lot, we all waved. That was the quietest ride home from the shore that I ever experienced.

WIWAK nobody, contrary to what some Boomers will tell you today, even knew where Vietnam was on the world map. It was almost like Pearl Harbor in the 40's. Most parents from that time will tell you they had no idea where it was, but the Japanese attacked all the same. In eighth grade a nun, Sister Immacula, told all the boys in the class that some of us would be going there (Vietnam) after high school. We thought the nun had overdosed on prayer. It turned out she was right and it wasn't long before every kid knew exactly where that little country was. Kids I played with on my street, and in organized sports, today have their names listed on that black wall in Washington, D.C

WIWAK competing in the All America Soap Box Derby in Levittown was a dream of many of the kids from our area.

WIWAK most cheap, junky toys and prizes were labeled "Made in Japan". We used to call such products "Made in Junk-Pan."

WIWAK women and girls could always count on boys and men to hold a door open for them. Such niceties were commonplace, and were welcomed by the fairer sex.

WIWAK girl's fashion was conservative. Penny loafers ruled the day, and skirts below the knees were fashion mainstays. Two-tone buck shoes and knee-high socks were popular among pre-teens. One-piece bathing suits were popular at the pool, although boys really loved the new bikinis the most. While we went to the shopping center in the late 60's to see a topless bathing suit on display at Pomeroy's, no sightings were ever reported at the pool.

WIWAK the event that changed our times forever was when President John F. Kennedy was shot in Dallas, Texas on November 22, 1963. Most Boomers know exactly where they were on that tragic day. It was the first and only time I ever saw a nun cry all over her clean habit.

WIWAK James Dean and Marilyn Monroe did it for every boy and girl in America. Other stars followed, but these two remain Hollywood royalty in our minds.

WIWAK Loony Tunes were the favorite cartoons, bar none. Every class clown could do some characters from the cartoons in his repertoire.

WIWAK those that picked up the bad habit of smoking quickly picked up typical smoker ways. Some imitated guys from the neighborhood, while others tried to pick up some of the mannerisms of TV and movie stars. The most disgusting trick was sucking the smoke up your nose immediately following a drag

WIWAK the biggest dance craze ever was the Twist by Philly's Chubby Checker. Even though the record had been done earlier, and some say better, by Hank Ballard and the Midnighters, most of us quickly learned to do the simple dance to Chubby Checker's version. Most kids laughed when they heard that people actually paid someone to teach them how to do one of the easiest dances of all times. If a dance was hard we used to teach each other how to do them. Some kids had no partners at home and taught themselves by using the corner of a wall, or swinging on a door knob or refrigerator handle.

WIWAK the word "atomic" was a big catch phrase used to sell every kind of product imaginable. Somehow we thought if a product had the word "atomic" in it then we were part of something futuristic.

WIWAK TV dinners and Tang made us feel like we were an integral part of the New Frontier. Everything now could be done in an instant. Anyone who made things the old way was considered old fashioned, even though grandmother's food was always tastier.

WIWAK Egyptian mummies in schools were all the rage. Why anthropologists were revered for being modern-day grave robbers was beyond many of us. That didn't stop us from walking like ancient Egyptians. We never worried about being dug up in the future by some beings from another planet. The only people who had to worry about being put on exhibit, we surmised, were prominent figures.

WIWAK half the United States population after World War II was 25-years or less. There were scarcely any old people in Levittown. Most kids' grandparents lived "back home." Few services existed for old people in this community built for the young. Everything in Levittown was essentially geared for young people and their ever expanding families.

WIWAK everybody seemed to have the same metal legged tables and chairs in their dining rooms. The table could be made larger by folding it out from the middle. The only problem with the Formica topped tables was that they required the combined strength of Superman, Popeye, and

Hercules to unfold them. It seems food and moisture that got into the middle seam of the table formed a rust and glue that was probably the basis for Super Glue later on.

Chapter 13

Boys Only

Family friend and Bucks County Courier Times Sports Editor, Dick Dougherty (left) and Author Mike Tasker (right) with their cigars.

"Boys, if you burn your butt, be
prepared to sit on the blister."
Old Dutch saying quoted frequently by Anna Tasker

WIWAK all the guys would get together and try to sing like their favorite groups. The best place to sing in Levittown was an underground tunnel at the Tullytown train station. Later, at a dance, or some teen hangout, the boys would offer their latest take on some moldy oldie. A favorite pastime for some guys was inserting suggestive lyrics into songs like "The Name Game" and "A Town Without Pity," among others. Over the years hours were spent trying to nail down all the lyrics to "Louie, Louie." We just knew there had to be some sinister message in the song.

WIWAK puberty was a bloody time for boys, too. Razor blades at the time were one step above an old scout knife. At the first hint of a milk catcher above the top lip, most fathers would march junior into the bathroom for his first shaving experience. Later, most boys would shave in the morning and then spend most of the bus ride to school trying to stem the flow of blood with bits of toilet paper.

WIWAK we spent hours trying to perfect the skill of cracking an imaginary egg on someone's head. I told you before we had a lot of time on our hands. This also answers what some youngsters ask their Boomer fathers, "What did you do with all that spare time, Dad, when there were only three channels on television and no computers?" Some guys became so adept at cracking the imaginary egg that you'd swear the egg oozing down both sides of your head was a real one. Championships were held and the top practitioner was revered throughout the neighborhood. The rest of us watched admiringly as the masters practiced their trade in "eggdomology".

WIWAK one ear-popping pastime that doesn't seem as popular today was the prodigious art of cracking knuckles. The bone-cracking masters of yesteryear could draw a crowd with their bony concerto. And, it didn't take long before a contest was called, to figure out who was the best in a knuckle-off. It was important to try to figure out who could crack every knuckle on both hands in the quickest amount of time. Becoming champ gave you status. MVP awards were always bestowed on the boy who could register the loudest cracking noise. Competing in such sport was brief for many because only a true master could get his knuckles to respond again and again. To the consternation of all the boys in the neighborhood, our champ happened to be a girl. Her finger-tugging talents left the boys in the dust; she was just that gifted. Some boys' knuckles eventually became gnarled from repeated attempts to dethrone our champ. Most practitioners developed the annoying habit of pulling their knuckles all the time. They reasoned they never knew where their next challenge was coming from. I often wonder to this day whether these tactile pulling champs of 45-plus years ago can manipulate two-ply toilet tissue, or navigate a fork from plate to mouth today.

WIWAK nicknames were a part of growing up for boys. Getting a moniker from the gang was considered "neat." On the other hand, some nicknames were more of a brand that would live in infamy. Some "neat" and not-so-neat names included the following: Scratch, Banana, Fuji, Johnny Angel, Boochie, Close Eyes, Mickey Karate, Big D, Yak, Rabbit, Don No-Talk, Froggy, Head Zeppelin, Pack, Top Cat (T.C.),

Weezie, Smelly Kelly, and Tree. People given the above names still respond to their nicknames today.

WIWAK some names meant to demean others were given based on how they looked, or what they did. These names were not meant to endear certain kids to others, but meant to inflict pain. Bullies pulled names from one TV show that was very successful, but whose characters' names you didn't ever want. The show was the Addams Family, which featured more than its share of freaks. Being called "Fester" pegged you as a real loser. Not too far behind were the names Pugsley, Morticia, Lurch, Gomez, Cousin It, and Thing! Another show most of us liked, but didn't want to be associated with when it came to nicknames, was the Andy Griffith Show. Who wants to be called Goober, Otis, Floyd, Gomer, Opie or Barney? There weren't too many takers. Anybody for Dr. Zorba (Ben Casey)???

WIWAK the lengths of shoelaces were adequate enough to tie shoes and sneaks properly. Boys didn't need three feet of laces on each Converse. But colored laces were all the rage with black leather jackets.

WIWAK hitchhiking was not considered the risk it is today. Boys walked everywhere they wanted to go, but weren't shy about sticking out the thumb for a ride. Destinations included the Levittown Shopping Center, lakes, schools, Delaware River, athletic fields, bowling alleys, and Philadelphia via the railroad station, to name a few. Those who wore military uniforms were always picked up by my uncles, all five of whom served in World War II. Military men would always stand with their bags at the entrance to the Pennsylvania Turnpike, and it wasn't long before they got picked up.

WIWAK knowing the name and year of any car was a talent most boys admired. We competed with each other to see who could name the model and year of each passing car. If you didn't know cars, you were viewed as odd. Any car worth noting then was American made.

WIWAK a discarded lawn mower offered the opportunity for aspiring mechanics among us to create a motorbike. We called those kids who could put together a motor bike motor-heads. Once the bike was assembled, we rode the bike up and down the streets until someone called to complain about the constant noise.

WIWAK most kids wore dungarees with cuffs, and anything floating around outside invariably wound up in our cuffs. We learned early not to lie down and put our legs over your heads after playing outside.

WIWAK most miserable, moody and creepy boys went on to become miserable, moody and creepy adults.

WIWAK after a fresh snowfall most boys searched for the largest sledding hill that would offer danger of getting hit by passing cars. I guess flirting with death is a boys' thing.

WIWAK rubbing snow in the faces of girls we liked was one way for us to show that we liked them. We believed we were smooth operators on those cold winter days.

WIWAK the boardwalk at the Jersey shore offered boys like us a unique way to pull a practical joke on people we lovingly referred to as Dollar "Bills." One of us would be chosen to slip beneath the boardwalk and stick a dollar bill halfway up through the wooden boards. Ninety-nine percent of the time it was a man who took the bait. For some unknown reason men always seemed to be looking down as they strolled along the boardwalk with their families in tow. As the man would bend over to pick up the bill, the prankster would yank the bill back down. For some reason we couldn't get enough of this and nearly died laughing. We'd rip a gut when some greedy marks would try to see through the crack.

WIWAK boys solved disputes by playing "Rock, Paper & Scissors".

WIWAK stuffing a whole pack of five-cent Bazooka bubble gum in our mouths at once was a great way to get giant bubbles, although it took some strong jaws to get the gum stick into shape before blowing. If you didn't want to blow bubbles, an alternate form of entertainment with the pink gob was taking it out of your mouth and twirling it around your fingers. After the gum lost its flavor, many kids would throw it on the ground and hope someone would step on the sticky mess.

WIWAK the most brazen prank some boys would pull on adults was the "Old dog poop camouflaged in the leaves trick." Fledgling pyromaniacs would do the following: get a pile of poop, place it at a cranky neighbor's door, cover it with leaves, light it and knock on the door.

WIWAK getting a new glove, bat, or baseball was special. Most young boys swore new equipment helped their game. These gifts from the sports gods usually arrived at Christmas, birthdays and graduations only.

WIWAK boys would recreate the hand of a mummy by dripping hot wax from a candle onto it. After the hand had become completely encased in the wax, the owner of the hand would chase girls to scare them. When the chase was over, all the guys would circle around and watch the hand break out of its wax encasement.

WIWAK the toy model industry took off in the mid 60's when they started making plastic model kits of all our favorite monsters, and different macabre events. My favorite was a model prisoner getting the blade of the guillotine, which actually worked. Other boys liked the usual monsters – Dracula, Wolf Man, and Frankenstein.

WIWAK weekends were reserved for fixing and sprucing up cars. Depending on the season, most car aficionados developed a modern day horse-cowboy relationship for the latest models coming out of Detroit. Cruising at night showing off the sparkling muscle cars was a weekend pastime. Taking time out and pulling into fast food parking spots by backing into them was also an integral part of meeting girls and guys in town. It also didn't hurt being noticed with toy dice hanging off rear view mirrors. We looked forward to being age 16 and owning our own wheels.

WIWAK most boys couldn't wait to go fishing with their dads, but some kids became totally frustrated the first time they went – their dads were always yelling at them. Their closed face reels usually made dad lose his patience. They were always jamming up when the fishing line got all jumbled up. Dads, who thought they were going to fish all afternoon uninterrupted, wound up fixing their sons' reels continuously. Those lacking patience with junior constantly ranted and raved at their kids. Some boys never forgot their one and only trip to the lake with dear old dad. After spending time with some dads, most boys would fish with boys.

WIWAK my friend, Ray, had an uncle who was in the Twilight Zone episode where Lee Marvin was a boxer. This gave my buddy instant status, and it rubbed off on us since he was part of our gang. Nobody was more macho in the movies in the 60's than Marvin, an ex-Marine. He was a man's man.

WIWAK sometimes 'friends' would get you involved in a caper you didn't want any part of. I foolishly accepted a swig of a bottle of warm 7-Up from a kid who swiped it from Pop's storage room at the corner store, even though I knew it was stolen. I'm sure my face was as red as the next kid I offered a swig to. I figured offering another boy a swig would make him an accomplice in the commission of a petty crime.

WIWAK many boys opened pop bottles with their teeth. Older teens could open up bottles on several different areas of a car, especially the door. Still, the most revered way of getting at a Coke was to open it with your teeth, even if an opener was available.

WIWAK boys would take out their big bags of green plastic army men and stage great battles outside in the dirt. Sometimes boys would light matches and melt the army men's arms to give them a new position. After the last shot had been fired and the battle was won, burying the dead would commence. Exhuming the participants the following day would give the soldiers another chance to fight the next war. But some men and army vehicles were never found and remain buried where the Boomers left them all those years ago in their childhood homes.

WIWAK cattails grew in the drainage ditches throughout the summer time. Boys would collect the weed and dry them out on their house roof. Once dried, they were lit to keep insects away. We also snipped off the stems and acted like we were smoking big cigars.

WIWAK tying a sled to cars and riding around our section was a lot of fun.

WIWAK there was always one boy pushing tall tales around school. Tales of Midnight Mary (a girl who drowned in a lake on her prom night), Crybaby Bridge (a bridge you can hear someone crying on if you stop in the middle of it) and Gravity Hill (car parked at bottom goes back up a hill on its own by force of gravity) were always being peddled around the neighborhood throughout the year. These yarns were very popular, and this was before drugs hit the scene. People always talked about them, but nobody ever wanted to find out for sure if they really existed. Like John Dillinger and his supposed physical contribution to the Federal Bureau of Investigation Building in Washington, D.C., none of these tales has ever been confirmed.

Chapter 14

Working for a Living

"Work!"
Maynard G. Krebs

WIWAK I couldn't wait for a real job that paid real money. After getting my working papers at age 14, I vowed to go to my favorite fast-food restaurant, Gino's, and stuff my face with cheeseburgers, fries and shakes with my first paycheck. As a young boy, I never seemed to get enough of Gino's. Ironically, it turned out that my first job was cooking the Colonel's Kentucky Fried Chicken in eight pressure cookers at GINO'S!!! There was a God, and he heard my prayers! Even though God never revealed the Colonel's special recipe to me, I was the happiest employee that ever walked through the doors of Gino's earning the princely sum of 90 cents per hour. But I quickly learned to watch what you wish for. The luster of the work world and the food it afforded quickly lost its shine. Like other Boomers in their first job, I set my sights on climbing up the corporate burger ladder. Figuring I could pull down a $1 per hour salary by the end of summer through hard work, I put my nose to the grindstone. Then, fate altered my aspiring career. My brother Charles got me tickets to see the Miracles, featuring Smokey Robinson, at the Camden County Music Fair in New Jersey. The choice seemed easy to make, after working all summer in the heat without one day off. However, my manager said he "needed me," and seeing Smokey and his gang would result in my immediate termination. I went with Smokey and never looked back. I went early to the show, and as luck would have it, I personally met Smokey Robinson and spoke with him for several minutes– Oooh Baby, Baby!

WIWAK I used to get money under the table by shining shoes in a bar before I went to work legally. The men at that time were always very aware of their language when a kid was in the bar. I had my own shoe shine box and always got more money than the 10 cents that I was charging.

WIWAK a bottle of Coke would take the rust off a nail and was good for cleaning out drains. It was also good for a two cent bottle return at the store.

WIWAK I used to wait outside a grocery store with my

friend, George, and ask women who were leaving if they wanted their bags carried to the car for 25 cents.

WIWAK we used to get a can of paint and draw the numbers of addresses in the neighborhood on the curb for 10 cents.

Chapter 15

A Day to Remember

Mike Tasker on shoulders of Cousin Billy.

"You can't live a perfect day without doing something for someone who will never be able to repay you."

John Wooden

WIWAK every group of kids has a mooch in it, and we were no different. Nobody could purchase anything to eat or drink without Slim asking for a "swig" or "piece."

For many, it was hard to eat something and wash it down with a Coke while someone stared at you with puppy-dog-eyes. Although there were one or two among us who could watch their favorite aunt or uncle die in front of them while feasting on something, many of us always gave in and gave Slim a share. It finally got to the point that one of the guys decided he was going to "cure" Slim of his disturbing habit of begging. Knowing that Slim would ask for a bite of a fresh bought hoagie, Joey decided to strategically place an Ex-Lax into the sandwich. Slim ate everything so quickly Joey was confident he wouldn't detect the chocolate surprise. Later that night, Slim exited the group for home early. The next day Joey told him what he had done, and Slim responded saying, "Joey, I had the runs so bad last night I think I set a world land speed record three of the seven times I raced to the bathroom! I kid you not! I also donated a pint of blood to the toilet gods during my agony!" Slim's butt returned to normal, but he never again asked anyone for anything. It's a day I'll never forget.

WIWAK there were a boatload of movies that scared the daylights out of us at the Towne theater on Saturdays. These flicks resulted in quite a few nights of sleeplessness. My older brothers would always assure me that the monster in the movie was coming to get us as we trekked home. After viewing Brides of Dracula with Peter Cushing as its star, my brother, Charles, told me Dracula was coming to get me that night as soon as the lights went out. I never went to the bed without the light on from that time forward. I still leave the light on today, but I'm sure it's just a habit. Today's kids think we were deranged to ever think such tripe was scary.

WIWAK nuns handed out justice quicker than anybody in the history of mankind. Do anything wrong and they'd give a solution to your misbehavior at school. Two boys I knew stole beanies off girls in school. Quicker than you can say, "Drag queens," they were both put in girls uniforms and displayed to all 16 classes in school. They both had posters attached to their blouses stating, "I'm a girl!" Neither boy ever borrowed another stitch of girl's clothing for the remaining nine years they spent in the eight year school.

Chapter 16

Odds-N-Ends

1950's Boys practicing yoyo tricks*

"I should have no objection to go over the same life from its beginning to the end: requesting only the advantage authors have, of correcting in a second edition the faults of the first."

Benjamin Franklin

WIWAK every student understood exactly what the Latin phrase "In loco parentis" meant. Together our teachers and parents would go loco on us the very day we caused any problems. Also, all of us believed in miracles, because we saw nuns and lay teachers control and successfully

* Photo - http://mousekevitz.livejournal.com   153

teach class populations of 98 pupils on a daily basis.

WIWAK my friends and I couldn't wait to get older and become teenagers. Contrary to accepted stereotypes in Hollywood movies depicting the era, boys and girls dressed up for school, dances and local events. The few kids that wore leathers, or looked like they just jumped out of bed, were exceptions. Finding the right dress or suit and primping for a dance on a Saturday night was a right of passage.

WIWAK an adult could draw a small crowd of kids watching him play with a model airplane that actually flew. We would sit and watch him fly his high priced toy for as long as he flew it. One time we watched a tethered plane actually snap loose and fly off into the distance with the hobbyist running after it in a high speed pursuit. The plane crashed and burst into flames 200 yards away. Those of us in his proximity had to try hard not to laugh in front of him.

WIWAK many of us couldn't get enough of Fizzies. Whatever happened to the long tube of colored sugar remains a mystery. Come to think of it, whatever happened to large tablets of Sweet Tarts?

WIWAK beatniks resembled something from outer space. Although the only beatnik most of us even knew was Bob Denver (Maynard G. Krebs), nobody went out and tried to emulate his "work" ethic. Maynard was one of the main characters on the 1950's hit "Dobie Gillis," who would be terrified if anyone asked him to work.

WIWAK the goofiest fad involved granny glasses and granny dresses. These glasses were colored and had small square lenses. We thought we looked neat in them. This was later followed by pet rocks.

WIWAK there wasn't a pizza store in every strip mall. As kids we used to think the mix we bought in a box was great.

WIWAK school photos were in black and white, as were team photos of the various sports teams we joined. Not much had changed from Abraham Lincoln's time 80-plus years earlier.

WIWAK America went into a photography kick, with all types of instant gizmos and molten hot flashbulbs. We would actually sit around the Polaroid camera waiting anxiously for the picture to develop. Once the photo appeared we had to brush it with some chemical that came with the film to preserve the picture. The house smelled like a photo studio. Fashioning bunny ears above somebody's head just as the picture was about to be snapped was a great trick with kids. Not only was it magic watching it appear on paper, but using a stick that resembled a long chapstick cylinder was part of the fun of preserving the picture for posterity. Some in our family really liked the smell of the lubricant that smelled like a cross between Vaseline and glue. I'm sure many kids in the 60's did something fiendish with these Polaroid sticks when mom and dad weren't looking.

WIWAK the one river used to gauge proper time was Old Man River – the Mississippi. Yet, as we got older and a bit more intelligent, some kids discontinued the practice when they found out that saying Mississippi was slightly more than one second in time. Kids could be as picky as adults. Some kids even got their own watches.

WIWAK I had my favorite marbles in a tin box. My cat's

eye marbles were my favorite and I only used some of them for tight games. Kids in the city were better marble players than most kids in the suburbs. Why? They didn't have as much space to play in on city streets.

WIWAK the only kid from Levittown who sang on corners and achieved 15 minutes of fame for his efforts was one of the kids featured singing on the corner in the first Rocky movie.

WIWAK an expeditious way to cool off on a 95-degree day was running after a street sweeper spraying water. Some kids would even jump on the back of the truck to get a ride to another part of the section.

WIWAK sitting around with best buddies perusing comic books or sharing kid novels was a great way to make the time fly by on a hot summer day.

WIWAK many mothers used inexpensive remedies passed down through the generations to cure us of minor maladies. The ingredients were right there in the pantry, the ground, or in a dressing drawer. One curious remedy that worked every time for earaches was filling a sock with warm salt and placing it around the ear. Two others were using mustard plasters for chest congestion and mud for bee stings.

WIWAK everything seemed to be a contest. When somebody got a typewriter, the newest contest was determining who could pound out sentences the quickest about a lazy fox. Parents would chime in and tell us that these skills, like Latin and shorthand, would later help us climb the ladder of success in the work world. Their crystal balls were about as accurate as our old Ouija boards and fortune 8 balls.

WIWAK I'd spend all Sunday morning reading and then copying cartoons with my Silly Putty.

WIWAK we received two papers out of Philadelphia – The Inquirer and The Bulletin. Life and Reader's Digest came in the mail. Most families loved to read back then.

WIWAK the largest car dealership in the world was located a few miles from our home – Reedman's. Knowing someone who worked for this dealership gave one instant status. Asking my friend's mother, who was a secretary for Ralph Reedman, what the owner was like intrigued us. It was "neat" to know someone who worked for a real, live millionaire.

WIWAK some kids liked to eat Vaseline, chew on a stick of butter, or eat hamburger raw – with salt on it, of course!

WIWAK an item we had plenty of during the summer months was "time." After playing every game imaginable, we were left with each other's thoughts. Even at a young age we pondered the existence of other life forms in the universe, and God Himself. When the evolution theories popped up many of us didn't seem to accept them. Though he had no theological training, one kid, Billy, felt Darwin's reasons were bogus, because if we were created in the image of the Almighty, then the ancestral monkeys had to be made in his image. We agreed Darwin was all wet and "we" resemble the Man upstairs. However, I still like eating bananas!

WIWAK Christmas was not given the politically correct name of Mid Winter Recess, nor was it given the nickname

Xmas.

WIWAK paddleball was a toy that required great hand-eye coordination. Like most toys, this toy always involved a competition. The ball always flew off eventually. I always aimed it at my brother just in case it would fly off.

WIWAK deaf and dumb children frequented a park we played in; it later became known as the "Deefies."

WIWAK summer was a time for fishing. Getting together the gang to fish local lakes, rivers, and canals was no problem at all. Preparations for the piscatorial adventure would usually begin the night before, catching night-crawlers, our primary bait. Catching the long worms took patience and talent. Getting a doubleheader, two worms stuck together procreating, was the sign of an expert. To us there was nothing more magical than seeing a ring of campfires around a lake prior to the opening of trout season. Making memories with fishing buddies on or near the water beat anything going on in our house, or on the boob tube.

WIWAK visiting Washington, D.C. and visiting any building open to the public could be done without passing through any maze of security and checkpoints. It was a very nice town back in the 60's.

WIWAK watermelon was a welcomed treat each summer. Kids who ate the sweet fruit were put into two categories: seed-eaters and seed-spitters. Parents gave stern warnings about watermelons taking root in our stomachs.

WIWAK walking out the door in the morning and not coming home until dinner time was a daily ritual with most of the gang. We never ran out of things to do, or kids to play with. We didn't need anybody to tell us what to do. The only check-in at home was if we were eating over someone else's house.

WIWAK we'd only ride a bicycle up to a certain age. Riding your Schwinn near age 16 was considered "un-cool." Big guys walked everywhere, or stuck the thumb out to get where they were going. We didn't have to worry about ending up on some whack job's dinner plate, or sliced, diced, and carved into pieces and put in a Kenmore deep freezer.

WIWAK beat sneakers ended up doing a high wire act as soon as we replaced them with a new pair of high-top "Cons" (Converse). Those worn out sneaks we once wiped off after each use remained on the wires until Mother Nature degraded them further. Sometimes an electrical employee from Philadelphia Electric stepped in and snatched them from their ignominious end.

WIWAK attaching old baseball cards to our bike's spokes gave our two wheelers the feel of a motorized vehicle. Some kids hooked balloons onto bikes, but they didn't last as long as cards. Steelworkers who worked the night shift didn't appreciate either model during daylight hours.

WIWAK having a split between your two front teeth gave you a leg up on others when it came to spitting. A split between made some girls quite attractive.

WIWAK countless softball and bowling teams were comprised of men who worked for the business embossed on their shirts. Businesses encouraged their young workers to join recreation leagues and play with their co-workers too.

WIWAK bikes were the preferred transportation to

get somewhere. Kids literally wore them out in a year, and found new shiny wheels under the Christmas tree.

WIWAK hucksters would come around the section in an open truck to sell fruit and vegetables. People welcomed these vendors, since many didn't drive cars yet.

WIWAK fun in the fall could be achieved by piling up a whole bunch of leaves. After making a mountain of leaves, diving into the foliage was a real treat. Having all the leaves in one place made it easy to deposit in an outside fireplace and burn them. Nothing beats the smell of leaves burning on a crisp autumn afternoon.

WIWAK there was no substitute for being first in whatever the gang did. We all believed in an old Yukon story: If you ain't the lead dog, the scenery never changes.

WIWAK tattoos were highly prized by kids, but ours were drawn on with ink by the artist in the gang. The only boys who had real tattoos in those days were ex-sailors from WWII and truck drivers.

WIWAK there was hardly a screen door in the neighborhood that wasn't pushed in from kids looking in over the years and asking parents if "Johnny could come out and play." A few parents prevented the practice with metal strips across the door. Those who didn't had a permanent indentation in their screen.

WIWAK there were certain adults all the kids liked because they didn't act like old fuddy-duddies. They didn't try to act like us, but they didn't act like they had one foot in the grave like most adults.

WIWAK a rope and chalk were all the materials girls

needed in a playground to keep them busy day-in, day-out. It also kept them in shape. Boys viewed jumping rope as something that was for girls only.

WIWAK visiting Santa Claus in Pomeroy's department store was magical. Nobody asked Santa for clothes, and he always came through with your favorite toy. On the other hand, the Easter Bunny never let anyone sit on his lap. Like all other things in Levittown there were always long lines to wait in. "Peter Cottontail" was always smiling, mute and only left us eggs, sticky chocolate eggs and clothes we didn't want. Long live Santa Claus.

Visiting Santa at Pomeroy's are Maureen (L), Peggy and Kathy Conroy

WIWAK football was a sport meant to be played in the snow, rain, sleet and slop. Some of the best games we ever played in were without pads and in a driving snow storm. When we finally finished, most of our clothes were soaked and in tatters. We really didn't feel the cold when we were young and having fun. Mom, however, didn't appreciate the ripped clothing.

WIWAK dressing to the nines as a small kid meant wearing a beaded Indian Belt and a Davy Crockett coon skin outfit.

WIWAK Little Leaguers looked forward to wearing their uniforms in a parade to start the new season each year. Those among us who sported new gloves and bats signed by

161

our favorite big league players drew a crowd of kids around them. Those who made the all-star team at the end of the season were awarded new hats and kids fawned over them as well.

WIWAK my brothers and sister had to pass their driving exam test at age 16 by actually using hand signals outside the driver's window. Having a state policeman accompanying teenagers during the test was a bit overwhelming and not many passed on their first try. Kids who flunked three times actually got other kids to take the driving test for them. These are the same kids that became proficient at opening a car with a clothes hanger, after leaving their keys in the ignition for the umpteenth time.

WIWAK a two story department store, not including basement, in the country's largest outdoor shopping center was a great place to get several kids together to play hide and seek. It was the mother of all hide-and-seek games. Store associates never bothered us because they were too busy selling merchandise to huge crowds daily. The center was a great baby sitter for children.

WIWAK most parents didn't have air conditioning in their cars, so windows were left opened and everyone's hair in the back became a royal mess. Kids spent a lot of time getting their hair just right. Subsequently, getting into a car always produced a fight for who sat in the front seat. Yelling, "Shotgun!" first usually secured the choice seat and saved your hair in the process.

WIWAK televisions and washing machines could be bought with coin slots attached to them. We were lucky enough to have a TV and a washing machine, but some people had to put quarters in each of them to get them running at their homes.

WIWAK high tech transistor radios were always smuggled into school at the end of September so baseball fans could listen to the playoffs and World Series. These small radios were the stuff of Dick Tracy and Flash Gordon. However, getting caught with one in school by the nuns would bring some old-time trouble with a capital "T".

WIWAK the cartoon gods cried the day television programmers put "Clutch Cargo" over the airwaves. This was a lame cartoon with real human mouths inserted into the cartoon.

WIWAK I had a large head. It was embarrassing to have to wear the coach's hat because they didn't have adjustable bands on the back of hats. There was one kid on the team who had a bigger head than mine and he didn't wear a hat at all. The local Little League had to make an exception for this boy.

WIWAK every activity we competed in had winners and losers. Unlike today, we learned very early in life trophies and prizes weren't handed out to every contestant.

WIWAK people used to dress up every time they went anywhere. Many places had dress codes and enforced them. Contrary to popular belief, dances for kids required dresses for girls and jackets and ties for boys. There were no "Fonzies" and "Pinky Tuscadaras" walking around a dance floor. People who looked like they just rolled out of bed were persona non grata and did not get past the door. Conformity was the name of the game and kids who didn't dress the part were not allowed in. Some kids sweated so much at dances that they would take an extra ironed white shirt with them. Girls wouldn't dance with some boys who were completely soaked when it was ladies' choice.

WIWAK George Washington, our first president, was a genuine American hero and his life was celebrated annually. Stores actually had legitimate sales and gave away free miniature cherry pies and candy. Sale items were unlike any others the rest of the year at stores in our town.

WIWAK the only time it was acceptable to lie in bed was Saturday. However, kids whose mothers wouldn't let them sleep came over our house to drag us out with them. Nobody had to be coaxed out on Saturday nights.

WIWAK every school had a rifle club to promote safety in handling firearms. Many of the men teaching the course saw action in WWII and the Korean Conflict.

WIWAK learning how to type on a manual typewriter was standard fare in schools. It didn't take long for kids to see who could type the fastest.

WIWAK some parents would make their kids go find a switch on a tree when they were bad. But quite a few parents had a cat-o'-nine tail hanging on the door hook in their kitchen for use on their kids. We didn't seem to hang around these adults much. Neither did their kids.

WIWAK everybody knew who was the heavyweight champion of the world. Not knowing the champ was considered un-American. Like baseball trivia, some kids could tell you anything you wanted to know about present and past boxers in any weight class.

WIWAK one could tell a nurse in a hospital from a female janitor by their white uniform, white hat and white stockings. Nurses dressed like nurses.

WIWAK I wanted to wear glasses like my best friend, Joe. I tried to flunk the eye test in school on purpose. Glasses, I felt, were good props for making faces like Joe's.

WIWAK we learned very early in life anything broken could be repaired. Rarely were things just thrown away. Everything from shoe soles to bikes was fixable.

WIWAK removing expended flash bulbs from cameras required quick hands. Quite a few kids got burnt handling them, and a lot of furniture got singed from those movie camera aficionados using "sun guns." As kids we swore the sun gun was actually brighter than the sun itself. It's always a blast to look back at films from the 50's and 60's with subjects shielding their eyes like some giant star in a galaxy was blowing up five feet away from them. It's not stretching the truth to say the wires guarding the sun gun nova actually glowed red after prolonged use. Besides almost burning down the house, disfiguring junior's hands for life, giving sis a permanent sun burn, and melting Poppop's eyes, the stun gun's passage into history came quickly because each use resulted in a 50 percent hike in the monthly electric bill.

WIWAK adults amazed me when it came to Christmas trees in the winter and charcoal fires on the grill in the summer. At Christmas, every man became an expert on how to set up a tree and care for it. Most adults I knew as a kid never stepped foot in the woods, but listening to them, you'd swear they'd come of age in the forest. In summer, most men would take over the cooking chores the moment it was decided that tonight's supper would come off the grill. Most men at that time couldn't cook themselves out of a paper bag, and they should have let Mom take care of business.

WIWAK it was just starting to become cool to have posters on the bedroom wall. Most kids had sports heroes and school pennants on their walls. In my bedroom it was a picture of Jackie Gleason shooting pool in a scene from the Hustler, along with a group shot of Smokey Robinson and the Miracles.

WIWAK moms ensured kids wouldn't lose their gloves by having kids wear mittens that snapped to their sleeves.

WIWAK going to the food mart was not like being in the city. In the beginning, there were no busses and the only two food stores were three miles away. My dad used to tell my oldest brother before he died he'd never forget going to the store. Taking a kid's wagon and setting off for the stores on a Saturday was a weekly ritual. That was 54 years ago when my dad helped settle a muddy new town called

Tom Tasker pulling wagon full of kids- sister, Jean- cousin, Timmy- Mike -midfifties.

Levittown. Not having a car in the family was not out of the ordinary for the early residents of Levittown. My mother only learned to drive after my father died.

WIWAK boys avoided getting beat up by relying on

their father or big brother. Small kids used this ploy often. I always used my brothers as a buffer against bullies that knew me. If the bully had no idea who I was, I told him my dad was right in the house and I would go get him if he didn't leave me alone. I'm sure my dad didn't mind.

WIWAK you knew something was good for you if they told you that a particular dish was "good-eating". Hunters and anglers would constantly use this terminology describing the palpability of certain fish and critters. Nobody in my immediate family believed then or now that liver was good-eating.

WIWAK some youngsters went all summer long without wearing shoes or shirts around the neighborhoods.

WIWAK I was so immersed in my private school upbringing that nuns looked ordinary to me and women with lipstick, hairdos, and dresses of the day looked like "painted women!" Nuns smelled fresh, looked clean, and were extremely mannerly. Eventually, I dreamed of nuns in my sleep where I got to see their real hair and became their best friend. I even found out in those dreams where they lived and what they looked like in regular clothes. The dreams were like being in the Holy Fortress of Solitude that Superman visited in the comic books of the time.

WIWAK I very much wanted to meet the characters John, Jean, and Judy (the Catholic equivalent of Dick, Jane and Sally in our readers) and hang out with them on a daily basis. Whenever I read about their lives, they seemed to have so much more going on than I did. Let's face it, their lives were in a book and everyone I went to school with knew them on a first name basis.

WIWAK playing war and westerns around Levittown neighborhoods sometimes involved dozens of kids. There was nothing greater than choosing sides, and then listening to cap guns blasting and kids arguing about who was dead, and who was not dead. Some participants also provided great death scenes in the middle of the battles. And then there were those kids who dressed up in army uniforms and western outfits. After an afternoon of killing one another, we'd talk about who did what to whom for hours on end. It was a magical time. None of the kids that took thousands of make-believe lives ever grew up to be real live murderers. These hombres had their fill of fake blood as kids.

WIWAK my brother, a friend, and I took our first and last trip to live in the woods without any adult supervision. Our plan was initially scheduled to be at least three days in length. We thought we had enough provisions and weapons to make a go of things. After building a fort, we realized we didn't have any matches to set a fire to cook our meager rations. We ate everything raw in one sitting. My brother tried to kill a squirrel with his bow, but lost both arrows in the brush. Next, it started to rain in the woods and we ran home wet and defeated from our five hour stay in the great outdoors. We never tried to stay in the woods again. I never enjoyed dinner like the one Ma cooked for us that night....

REGARDLESS of where Boomers grew up, this generation was unlike any that has come before or since. These kids were allowed to be kids, by parents who had a lot of their youth taken away from them during the Depression and World War II. These parents were determined to win for their kids a childhood that they never had. Many Boomers grew up spoiled, and some still wonder now what they're going to do when they grow up. Nonetheless, Boomers created for the generations that have followed them many scientific and technical wonders. The "experts" said we would never be able to compete with other countries in the future. The experts were wrong then, and are wrong now, as they still try to figure out what the Boomers will do next. Boomers continue to reinvent themselves and challenge all the stereotypes of old age. Overwhelming numbers avoided becoming replicas of mom and dad in conforming to expected standards. They refused to "act their age" at every stage of their development and still refuse to simply fade away and let the old rocking chair grab them. Boomers have always been creative, especially when it came to filling up each day of their lives. Some of the things on the previous pages continue to be done today by children, but many of the goings-on the Boomers came up with have never been, nor should be, replicated.

Looking back reminds this amazing generation their future will most likely be written by their collective

hands, not by the know-it-all talking heads that pontificat
24-7 on the boob tube. It will be a long time befor
historians give a true assessment of Boomer impact i
the 20th and 21st centuries. If the truth be told, the futur
that remains for them awaits their unique imprint on
as well. They remember what the "Greatest Generation
told them over and over again: "If you want, you can!"

"Say goodnight, Gracie."
"Goodnight, Gracie."
R.M.A.
m.e. tasker

Photograph Notes

Most of the photos in this book were donated by the Tasker Family. No copyright is intended for any photos used in the book and Mystical Rose Press thanks all owners of copyright for their use.

Photo Credits

Page 4 -Urban Archives,Temple University

Page 30 -From the Jerry Blavat Collection

Page 41 -U.S.Civil Defense Instructional Film, "Duck and Cover," starring "Bert the Turtle."

Page 62 -The Mount Carmel Academy, Archdiocese of New Orleans.

Page 66 -David Laambert
"Our Dance in the DDT," http://southernersjournal.com

page 78 -LPRA Pool in Levittown,Pa.-Courtesy of Bucks County Library Levittown Room Archives.

Page 79 -Courtesy of Joe Marazzo
http://www.deliciousicecream.com

Page 80 -Early Levittown and Beyond website
by Frank Barning and Friends.

Page 95 -Courtesy of Victoria Pirolli.

Page 97 -http://www.tvcrazy.net

Page 103 -Joe Munroe, Ohio Historical Collections

Page 127 -http://www.wikipedia.com

Page 153 -http://mousekevitz.livejournal.com